DIY *with* JAY

DIY *with* JAY

JAY BLADES MBE

bluebird
books for life

First published 2022 by Bluebird
an imprint of Pan Macmillan
The Smithson, 6 Briset Street, London EC1M 5NR
EU representative: Macmillan Publishers Ireland Ltd, 1st floor, The Liffey Trust Centre,
117–126 Sheriff Street Upper, Dublin 1, D01 YC43

Associated companies throughout the world
www.panmacmillan.com

ISBN 978-1-5290-9128-1

1 3 5 7 9 8 6 4 2
A CIP catalogue record for this book is available from the British Library.
Printed and bound in Italy.

MIX
Paper | Supporting
responsible forestry
FSC® C116313

Publisher Carole Tonkinson
Project Editor Katy Denny
Production Manager Sarah Badhan
Art Direction and Design Nikki Dupin, Studio Nic&Lou
Prop Styling Andi Redman

Always read and follow safety instructions supplied by manufacturers of tools and materials, and
follow all accepted safety procedures. The information in this book is intended as a general guide
and does not substitute for professional advice for your specific projects. Pan Macmillan accepts no
responsibility for any damages or injuries suffered as a result of following the information given in this book.

Visit www.panmacmillan.com to read more about all our books
and to buy them. You will also find features, author interviews and
news of any author events, and you can sign up for e-newsletters
so that you're always first to hear about our new releases.

As many people will know, especially anybody who saw the BBC documentary *Jay Blades: Learning to Read at 51*, I am severely dyslexic. To make this book happen, I worked with Ian Gittins, my ghost-writer from my autobiography, *Making It*, and Katy Denny. They helped me to get everything in my head down on paper, but I can assure you of this: the ideas are all mine!

Introduction

10

18

DIY
Basics

Kitchen

48

84

Hallway
&
Stairs

150

Living
Room

118

Bathroom

Bedroom

232

*Index
&
Thanks for
Reading*

190

Outdoor
Spaces

266

DIY is intimidating, if you don't know how to do it. And if nobody has ever shown you, why should you know?

DIY is a funny thing. What's it all about, anyway? Well, let's look at the phrase. DIY: Do It Yourself. All it means is that, when there are jobs and repairs that need doing around the house, you do them yourself rather than getting someone in. When you strip it down, most DIY is common sense – yet many people are terrified of it.

I understand that. I get it. DIY is intimidating, if you don't know how to do it. And if nobody has ever shown you, why should you know? I guess I am regarded as a bit of a DIY whizz nowadays and yet, if I am honest, I was a bit of late starter myself.

Most people first discover whether they are any good at practical stuff in woodwork lessons in school. Not me! As I said in my autobiography, *Making It*, I was in the 'L' [lower] stream at secondary school and the teachers hardly bothered to teach us anything. We certainly never got woodwork classes!

The teachers' basic thinking was that they wouldn't let us 'L' kids near anything sharp, like a saw or a chisel, or anything with a flame, like a Bunsen burner, in case we attacked them, or tried to burn the whole

school down! So unfortunately there were no early DIY lessons for Jay!

When I was a kid, with no dad around, my mum always said I was the man of the house, but she stopped short of giving me any DIY jobs to do. I think that was pretty wise! I'd had no role model to show me what to do. The last thing she needed was me wrecking the place.

When I moved out and started living on my own, my DIY activities were also pretty limited by the fact that I didn't have any tools. With no dough, I couldn't afford a hammer, or a drill, or a saw, so I had to work with stuff that I could fasten together without any equipment.

Old milk crates always came in useful. They were very robust, so I'd get hold of a few and stack them up. They were designed to interlock together, so I stacked up two piles and stuck a couple of planks across them. Bosh! There was my bedroom shelving!

If I needed a unit to hang my clothes in, I'd find a few breezeblocks lying around, stack them up and lay a scaffolding pole or broomsticks across the top. Voila! An instant

wardrobe! It might have been rough and ready, but it did the job that I needed it to.

I've always been into make-do-and-mend and my early DIY adventures were all about that. I'd use pallets for a bed base, or put big cushions on top of them to make a sofa. I'd mix stuff I'd found lying around with gear I got dirt-cheap from charity shops. It didn't stop it all looking great!

Now, don't worry! My skills and know-how have come on since those days. I'm not about to advise you to go out and prowl the streets by your gaff looking for milk crates or random breeze blocks! I'm a bit more refined nowadays – and I want to share some of my knowledge.

DIY with Jay is going to walk you around your house and give you tips for every room – and for your outside spaces, too. Are you looking to re-tile your bathroom or add extra cupboard space to your kitchen? Or maybe you're keen to wallpaper your living room or totally revamp your hallway?

Whatever you need to make your home perfect for you and your family, there will be plenty within the following pages to help you. And not just practical step-by-step methods for some of the more popular techniques – I'm going to get your grey matter working hard to figure out what will work for YOU and your home. Because the way I like my gaff set up won't be the same as your ideal living space! It's worth the hard thinking time though, because when you have a clear vision of the overall look that you love and practical needs such as storage, you will be able to create a home that you truly love.

You know the thing you need most to start doing DIY? Confidence. A lot of people give up before they even start. They feel inadequate and are just too embarrassed to ask for help when it comes to basic stuff like how to put up a shelf or replace a cracked tile.

I get that, but you know what? Logically, it makes no sense. Nobody feels ashamed of sending their car to be serviced by a professional mechanic. They will happily hand the keys to a geezer in a garage who will sort it out for them, and wouldn't feel inadequate for not being able to do the work themselves.

Fair enough . . . yet these same people often feel like they've let themselves down when they have to hire a tradesperson to fix something in their house. They think they should be able to do DIY and repair their own home, yet why should they? Nobody has ever shown them how to do it!

I think it's natural for people to feel scared of tackling tricky-seeming DIY tasks. Even I get a bit worried going into certain jobs. You only feel OK if you know what you are doing – and, hopefully, that is where *DIY with Jay* comes in.

I'm lucky enough to make my living now by designing and repurposing furniture, presenting TV programmes – and helping people to repair stuff (you may even have heard of a little telly show I'm in!). I've picked up a lot of tips along the way, but I've never lost sight of one thing.

It's this: most DIY is pretty basic. If you're putting a shelf up, it needs to be level or things will fall off. If you're constructing a cupboard door, everything needs to be in line or that door will never shut! The point is that with a bit of know-how, it's all a lot easier than it looks.

I've learned that great, effective DIY is all about common sense and applying yourself.

Most DIY is pretty basic. The point is that with a bit of know-how, it's all a lot easier than it looks.

You don't need to be super-intelligent. It makes me laugh – there are people earning millions of pounds a year trading in the City of London who can't even wallpaper a room!

Honestly, there are companies in London now who charge these high-flyers exorbitant sums to teach them basic home maintenance. This book will do the same for you at a fraction of the price. Trust me, you're getting a bargain!

Do you want to get a dowdy bathroom looking as chic as one in a top-of-the-range hotel? Does your flagging boudoir need a rethink, and giving a bit of oomph? Or are you scratching your head and wondering how you can make the most of your back garden or other outdoor space?

Well, one good thing about me is that I'm rarely short of ideas. I'm going to give you plenty to be getting on with and, most importantly, explaining how to make them a reality. I'm going to give you the – here comes that word again – confidence to tackle jobs, both big and small.

Oh, and before I wrap this up and start giving you practical advice, there's one more very important thing I want to say: DIY should be fun.

No, really! You might find this hard to believe now but, when you get in the right frame of mind, doing DIY can be brilliant. When I start a job at home, I always get some soul or reggae music playing. I get nice and relaxed, and everything goes so much better.

The other amazing thing is that doing DIY, and doing it well, gives you so much satisfaction. You put down your screwdriver, look around you and think, that looks great – and I did it! I made my home better! You may not have experienced that feeling yet, but, believe me – you'll love it when you do.

So, let's get cracking! We'll learn as we go along. I am going to talk you through everything carefully, stage by stage and step by step. We'll hopefully even have a few laughs along the way! And let's start off by getting you sorted with the tools you're going to need to get to know . . .

The other amazing thing is that doing DIY, and doing it well, gives you so much satisfaction. You put down your screwdriver, look around you and think, that looks great – and I did it! I made my home better!

You may not have experienced that feeling yet, but, believe me – you'll love it when you do.

Basics

Jay's *Top Ten* Tools

These are the tools I am rarely without. If I'm doing anything in the house, or in my workshop, I always need at least some of these everyday heroes. Before you go rushing out to buy new tools, though – especially if they're on the pricier end of things, like a drill – ask around and see if any of your friends or family have one you could borrow. And even if you don't have the exact right tool for the job, think laterally. I'll 'fess up: I've been known to use a handy table knife when I can't lay my hands on my screwdriver!

1 PENCILS

Pencils are necessary for pretty much every DIY job: marking where to position something, where to cut something, or where to drill or hammer. Mind you, it's best to keep a few handy, as they tend to go walkabout.

2 TAPE MEASURE

Measure twice, cut once! I can't stress enough how important it is to measure things properly. That way, you can plan efficiently, make things to fit the space, or calculate exact quantities for things like tiles and wallpaper. Make sure you have a sturdy, retractable tape measure. They don't get tangled up.

3 LEVEL

Listen up: there's no point putting up a shelf if everything is going to roll off it because it's slanted! Luckily, there are plenty of handy gadgets to help you get this right. There are free smartphone apps or you can buy laser levels that emit a beam to use as your straight line. Or, go old-school with an old-fashioned spirit level which has an air bubble inside liquid.

4 SMALL CRAFT HAMMER

These are quite useful for more delicate work when you are using little pins or tacks. You don't always want a big, heavy hammer.

5 BIG EVERYDAY HAMMER

However, there are times when you DO want a big, heavy hammer to give a job plenty of welly! The most common type is a claw hammer, which has one side of the head that's flat for bashing nails in, and the other side with a curved 'claw' for pulling nails out.

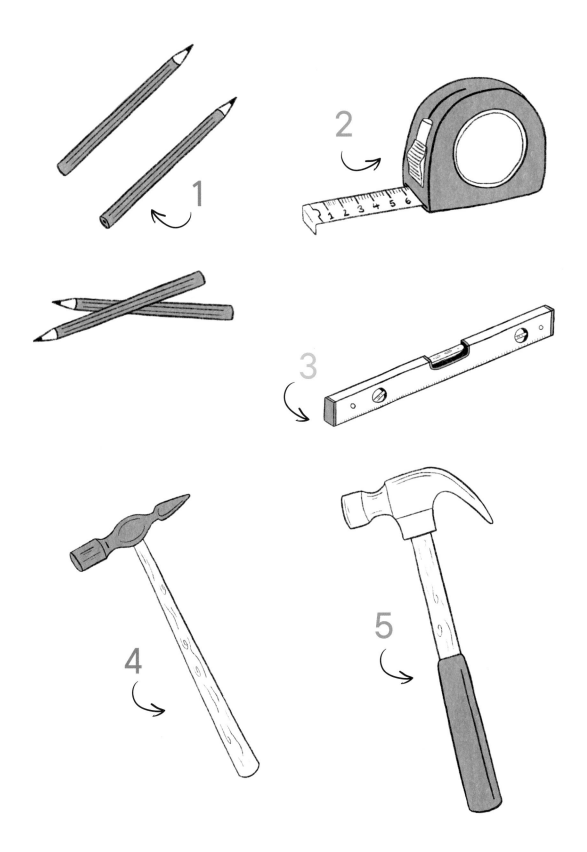

6 SPANNER / WRENCH

Adjustable ones are the most versatile and even these come in a range of sizes. You need a wrench to tighten or loosen bolts, nuts or pipes.

7 DRILL

You definitely need a decent drill, and a selection of different drill bits. Cordless drills are best: they're easier to use and manoeuvre in tricky or tight spots, and you don't have to worry about cables or being near a power point. Remember: drill bits will get blunt over time and need replacing.

8 SCREWDRIVER

If you've got a decent screwdriver, it'll save you time on loads of jobs, big or small – especially if you use an electric one. Most modern ones come as a set with a variety of interchangeable heads to fit different sizes and types of screw, and a switch on the handle that means you can easily screw in either direction using a ratchet mechanism.

9 SMALL LIDDED CONTAINERS

You might think these are only for the kitchen – but think on! See-through containers with lids, such as old jam jars, are invaluable. I'm always losing screws and bits and bobs: they end up going everywhere. So, store them in something see-through. Perfect!

10 MAGNET

For some reason, you don't usually find a magnet in 'essential tools' lists. Well, it's essential for me! If you drop a screw, nail or other small metal bit down a crack, it can be a nightmare . . . especially when you manage to get it with your fingers only to drop it again! A magnet can be a superhero in this situation.

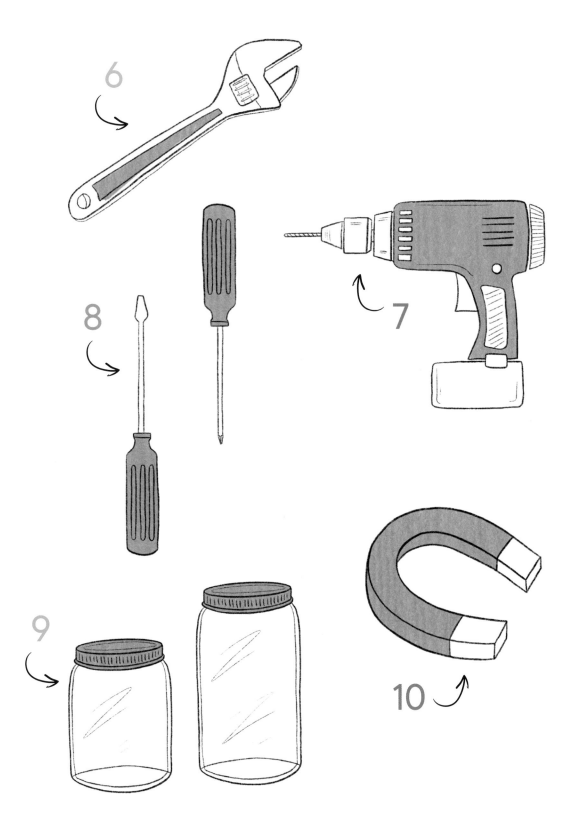

6

7

8

9

10

Hand Tools

So, you've got the essential kit! It should provide you with the tools you need for the majority of your DIY jobs. However, there are a few other useful bits to add to your toolbox as you get more skilled around the home.

---

1 STAPLE GUN
No, not the ones your teachers used to make mini booklets! These are bigger bits of kit that are useful for more heavy-duty jobs and materials. They're great for stapling fabric to frames and for securing insulation sheets within floor and wall voids. You can get these as manual versions or electric. Both do the same job but the powered version doesn't need quite so much muscle power.

2 UTILITY KNIFE
The best-known utility knife is the Stanley knife. These heavy-duty knives have retractable, general-purpose blades that make light work of little jobs like sharpening a pencil, or bigger ones such as trimming lino, underlay, carpet, or even wallpaper.

3 PLIERS
Get a decent set that includes combination pliers and long-nosed pliers. Combination pliers are useful for a variety of jobs, including gripping, twisting or even cutting wires. Long-nosed pliers are good for bending and gripping nails and wires and reaching into smaller spaces.

4 PROPER DRESSMAKING SHEARS
My favourite shears belonged to a tailor. I helped his elderly widow move into sheltered accommodation and she gave me her late husband's big dressmaking shears as a thank you (as well as a lot of his fabric for making suits). I love these shears, I use them all the time and I will keep them forever.

So many things are replaceable but the sentimental value means these are not. When they get a bit blunt or loose, I get them serviced and sharpened, and bosh! They're as good as new again!

5 SCRAPER AND PUTTY KNIFE

These are really useful for filling in cracks with all types of filler and for removing old wallpaper or paint. There is a slight difference between the two; scrapers have a stiff blade, while putty knives have a more flexible blade, suitable for getting filler into those awkward areas.

6 PLUMB BOB AND STRING

Talk about learning from history! This bit of kit dates right back to the ancient Egyptians building their pyramids. A 'plumb bob', which is a weight, is attached to a length of string then dropped down. Once the swinging string comes to a halt, it gives you a perfectly vertical line you can mark out. Thank you, Cleopatra (and gravity)!

7 CHALK LINE TOOL

Whether you're nailing battens or cutting vinyl, carpet, underlay or other materials, this tool is brilliant for marking out a straight line. You run the chalk-coated string along the line you want to mark, then pull it tight and pluck the string sharply. Voila! A chalk line just where you need it!

8 TILE-CUTTER

In any project, there will always be some tiles that need to be cut to fit a space. For simple, straight cuts, you can use what's known as a 'jig'. This scores the tile with a sharp cutter and then you can snap it apart along the line. For thick tiles, you'll need a heavy-duty jig. But if you're trying to cut tiles to fit around light switches or corners, i.e. doing fiddlier cuts, you should buy or hire an electric tile-cutter for greater accuracy.

9 HAND SAWS

As a kid, you probably saw these good old traditional saws hanging up in your grandparents' shed or garage. They're just as useful today. They are a cheaper alternative to power saws and are available with various handles and blades all suited to particular jobs. These range from the hacksaw for plastic and metal to the larger (but flexible) blade of a universal wood saw, used for timber.

10 STUD/CABLE DETECTOR

This is an excellent little gadget that is really useful to prevent you accidentally drilling or hammering nails into cables or pipes. It can detect fixings on stud walls, too.

Power Tools

Let's face facts. Sometimes, power tools outdo hand tools when it comes to doing a job quicker, with less sweat, and more accurately. Electric tools are expensive to buy, but if you're regularly doing DIY, a few key pieces are worth the investment. Here's an idea: spread the tools among friends and family and swap them between yourselves. Or, hire them as you need them, so you don't have to worry about storage or maintenance.

---

1 SANDERS

Sanding down woodwork can be a lot of hard graft, particularly when you're faced with large areas like whole floors. For these bigger spaces, it's worth hiring a belt or upright drum sander to make light work of the job. Edging sanders and disc sanders are useful for the edges of rooms, walls and smaller areas. Battery-operated sanders are much easier to work with as there are no wires to get tangled up while you're sanding small areas in different directions. This is less of an issue when you are sanding large areas.

2 HEAT GUN OR BLOWTORCH

If you'd rather not use chemicals and you want to get right back to the wood, a heat gun or blowtorch is your best bet for stripping paint. Be careful: always follow the safety instructions, and make sure you wear goggles and heatproof gloves. You will need to scrape away at the hot paint with the paint scraper to remove it all. Heat guns do the same job as a blowtorch but run less of a risk of scorching the wood (important if you're hoping to varnish the natural wood rather than repaint it) or causing a fire.

3 HANDHELD CIRCULAR SAW

This is a lightweight saw that's not too expensive and is good for cutting both curved-linear and straight lines in wood, plywood and MDF.

4 JIGSAW

With the right blades attached, these clever blighters can cut through metal, wood, plastic, laminates and ceramic tiles. The narrow blades make them great for cutting curves and awkward shapes.

5 MITRE SAW

A mitre saw is good for making cross and angled cuts in wood, plastic and metal. Ideal for jobs like cutting skirting boards or door frames so the edges meet cleanly.

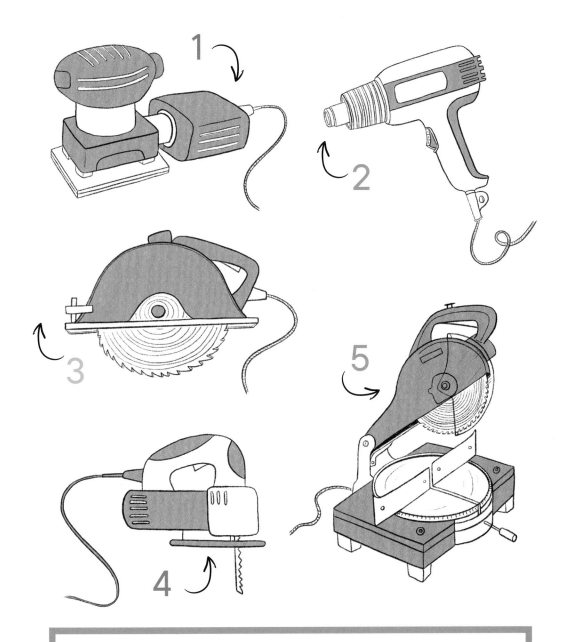

ELECTRIC SAWS

Power saws are essential for those jobs that a hand-held saw can do, but will take time and hard graft, or for really hard materials like metal or masonry. They can be cordless or mains-powered, and come in a wide range of types appropriate for different jobs, with a variety of blade diameters depending on the thickness of the material you want to cut. As I said earlier, they're safest with no cable, eliminating the risk of cutting through it and ending up in A&E!

Nails, Screws & *their* Cousins

Nail or screw? It can seem like they do the same job, and it's true that they are pretty interchangeable for some tasks. However, there are a few differences that will help you to decide which to use when.

Screws are a better option for temporary jobs as they're easier to remove than nails. For either option, though, it is important to check the walls for pipes and cables before you screw or nail into them, and ideally search for studs to provide support.

---

1 NAILS

There's a nail for pretty much every job. They are mostly used for larger projects when they are needed en masse, such as along joists or for nailing plasterboard or flooring, as they tend to be stronger and less expensive than screws. Use sturdier, longer nails for securing larger joins and for thicker materials such as plasterboard and large timbers, but turn to smaller nails and tacks for upholstery work and smaller joins. Nails are easy to insert by hand with a hammer or using a nail gun, and the heads can be hammered flush with the surface of the material you are nailing.

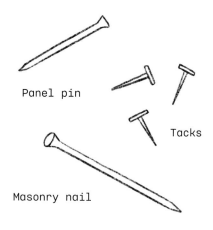

Panel pin

Tacks

Masonry nail

2 SCREWS

Screws are best for smaller projects such as woodworking and fixing hinges. Get a good mix so you have a variety of sizes and lengths for different purposes. Keep them separate or in a big box with compartments if you can, so you can always find the right size when you need it. Screws require a little more work to affix than nails, and you often need to drill a pilot hole first, but an electric screwdriver will do the hard yards for you.

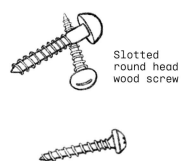

Slotted round head wood screw

Pan head chipboard screw

3 WALL PLUGS

These little plastic plugs are a life-saver if you're screwing into a brittle material or into a structure that might not support weight, e.g. when you're hanging pictures. To fit them, first drill a hole in the material, using the correct size of drill bit for the plug, then insert the plug into the hole. You can then screw into the plug, which will grip the screw and expand slightly into the surrounding wall. This will create a really strong joint and protect your wall from damage.

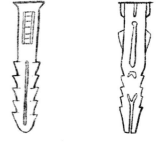

4 PLASTERBOARD FIXINGS

Plasterboard can be brittle so if you want to hang a picture or similar off a plasterboard wall, you will probably need more robust fixings than a nail or screw. Plasterboard fixings are also known as drywall fixings, are really easy to fit, and provide better support.

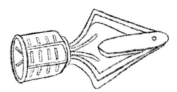

5 HOOKS

Hooks have so many uses around your home, hanging up anything from dog leads and keys to pictures or mirrors – and they come in an equally wide range of sizes and shapes. The size you use depends on the weight of the object you want to hang from it. Pictures or mirrors will hide the hooks behind them, but hooks for coats tend to be more visible so you may want to make them more aesthetically pleasing.

Materials & Surfaces /

Having a good basic understanding of the materials you are using is a real help when it comes to knowing how to fix them together. Knowing what you are drilling into will help you to know which fixings you will need to use, as well as the appropriate drill bits and lengths of screws or nails. It's a good idea to buy a stud detector for these jobs, as well as a cable detector, to make sure you don't damage any essential services, such as pipes or cables.

Here are a few of the materials that you will most commonly encounter in your home:

- **BRICKS**

  The most basic material of all. Bricks have been popular since the year dot for oodles of reasons. They come in a wide variety of colours and materials and look good, which makes them a great choice for external and internal walls alike. They're practical, absorbing humidity and thus minimizing the risk of mould or mildew. They're fire- and weather-resistant but also retain heat and are low maintenance, as you don't need to regularly paint or clean them.

  'Is there a downside, Jay?' you ask. Well, yeah, one: they're expensive, so if you're on a budget, you might prefer to look at other materials, especially for larger areas. If you are patching up an old wall in your gaff, use reclaimed bricks. They'll look a bit more weathered than new ones.

- **BREEZEBLOCKS**

  These are aerated concrete blocks that are used in large construction projects for all foundations and for external walls. They are really good insulators and are very durable, and although they feel lightweight, they are surprisingly solid. They're a less expensive option than bricks because they are larger and you need fewer of them to build a similar size of wall. They are not too pretty to look at, though, and should be rendered (skimmed over with plaster) for a more finished look. Some people like to use pebbledash for a more textured appearance.

- **LINTELS**

  A lintel is a beam placed above windows, doors or any other opening in a wall. It supports the weight from the structure above it, transferring the weight to the sides of the opening: literally, it's spreading the load! Lintels are generally made from concrete or granite, but sometimes they are strong timbers. Make sure you know exactly what you have before you start trying to fit curtain poles or blinds above windows. You can drill small holes into lintels without compromising their strength, but they can be tough and so you definitely need the right drill bit for the job.

- **PLYWOOD**

This is a board, or 'sheet' as it's known in the trade, made from three or more thin layers of wood glued together. These layers are known as 'plies', hence plywood. The more layers, the thicker the board. Plywood is a strong material that does not warp or crack, and there are different types for interior and exterior use. It's a really versatile material and is used for wall and floor coverings and furniture. It can also be bought as flexible sheets, which are good for curved structures. Oh, and get this: the strongest forms of marine plywood, which are designed to survive exposure to moisture, are used in aircraft and boat building! Wear a mask when cutting or sanding it.

- **CHIPBOARD**

Like plywood, chipboard is an engineered sheet of wood, made from wood chippings bound together using synthetic resin. It is popularly used for boxing in insulation, pipe work and cables, ceiling and wall fittings, and even as flooring. It can also be used to make furniture. Chipboard is best for indoor use as it won't withstand the outdoor elements in the long term. Wear a mask when cutting or sanding it.

- **HARDBOARD**

Another engineered wood option, made from compressed exploded wood fibres. This lightweight, flexible board is really versatile and works as a good substitute for wood. You can use it for anything from backing furniture to partitions and lining floors.

- **MDF**

MDF is a really popular sheet material. Why? It's cheap, easy to cut and holds its shape well. It comes in different thicknesses so there is usually a perfect type for whatever job you need it for. One word of caution, though: because it's made from wood fibres and solvents, you shouldn't inhale the dust that flies up when it is sanded or sawn. Always wear a mask when cutting or smoothing MDF, and never burn it.

- **INSULATION MATERIALS**

Insulating your home is a proper sensible move. It reduces heating bills and thus the excessive use of fossil fuels that contributes to climate change. So, fitting out your home helps your wallet and saves the world! What's not to like? The common forms of insulation material are fibreglass, which comes as a roll of material that can be cut to fit, and cellulose, a green option made from recycled paper, wool, straw and hemp. For maximum effect (and winter warmth), fit insulation in walls, attic spaces, ceilings and floors.

- **PLASTER**

Plaster comes as dry gypsum, lime or cement powder. It is mixed with water to create a stiff but workable paste that is applied to walls and ceilings to make a clean, smooth surface for painting over or wallpapering. Plastering is a bit of an art form and needs a whole lot of practice to get right. If you're aiming to plaster whole rooms, it might just be a job for the professionals! If you live in an old building, it might be that your existing plasterwork is made from lime or clay, which is much softer than modern types. You'll need to bear this in mind when fixing anything to the walls: wall plugs will be your friend here! By contrast, modern plaster is much more robust and durable.

Walls & *what they're made of*

I can't stress this enough: it's important to know how your walls are built. This is true if you're attempting to fix stuff to them, and even more so if you intend to do bigger DIY jobs, such as knocking through rooms to create more space. The walls could well be supporting other areas of your home and you don't want the whole thing to come crashing down on you!

As we become more aware and better at protecting our planet, it's also essential to know what green options are out there if you're putting up new walls or partitions.

EXTERNAL WALLS

These are the walls that face the outside elements. Because of this, these are made of solid, very hardwearing and weatherproof materials such as bonded bricks or concrete blocks. Some more rural or historic properties can be made from local natural stone.

Such walls are often cavity walls, which are two walls with a space between them. This gap prevents moisture entering your home and provides another layer of insulation, which will help to reduce heating bills.

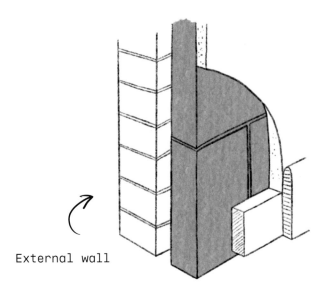

External wall

INTERNAL WALLS

There are two types of internal walls: party walls, which are the ones that divide you from your neighbours in terraced or semi-detached properties; and partition walls, which divide up the rooms inside your house.

Some of these may be what is known as load-bearing walls. It's crucial that you know whether they are before you knock any down, as these will be supporting the weight of a floor, the roof structure or even a chimney breast.

If you want to remove a section or the whole of a load-bearing wall, please, talk to a professional! You will need to insert a beam that is strong enough to take the weight of whatever is above it, unless you want to reduce your home to a pile of rubble (spoiler alert: you don't).

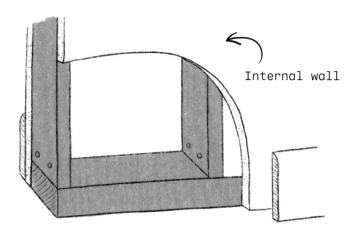

Internal wall

GOING GREEN

As we get ever more aware of the effects of climate change, we are all thankfully moving towards more sustainable forms of building and insulating our homes. There are loads of eco-friendly construction materials from sustainable sources available, such as bamboo, sheep's wool, straw bales and hemp blocks, or you can make use of recycled or reclaimed materials such as steel or wood. Get some professional advice from 'green' architects or builders on what works for your home and your budget.

Floors & *what they're made of*

You walk on it every day and yet you never give it a thought. But do you know what your floor is actually made of? Well, here's a quick lesson, and pay attention at the back!

In most buildings, floors are constructed using wooden joists. This is where timber struts are suspended between walls so that the flooring sits on top of a void. This space allows air to circulate beneath the building, and is a handy area to run and secure cables and pipes out of view.

The same structure gets used on the ground floor and on upper floors. Occasionally, ground floors or basement floors can be made out of solid concrete. This is a much cheaper way of creating a base, and just requires a layer of hardcore (coarse rubble), which the concrete gets poured over.

Why do you need to know what your floor is made of? Because it impacts how you lay your flooring on top of it. With wooden floors, it is easy simply to nail boards on top of the joists and then to lay any other flooring – carpet, vinyl, solid wood flooring and their required underlay – on top and fasten them down with screws or nails.

For concrete floors, underlay is also needed beneath vinyl or carpet, which should be glued down rather than nailed. Conversely, any wood flooring must be laid on top of a base of plywood sheets, onto which you can nail and secure the wooden boards.

Of course, a floor that's any higher than ground level will also have another job – as a ceiling! So, the joists supporting the floor will have a layer of plasterboard on the underside to hide them from view. This also serves to hold in any wiring or pipes so they are out of the way and out of sight.

Floor void: Opening left between joists in the floor that allows services such as pipework, ducts and cables to be laid and secured and hidden out of the way, protected by floorboards

Joists: timbers that run between the beams to provide a supportive frame for the flooring

Flooring: wooden boards, underlay and carpet

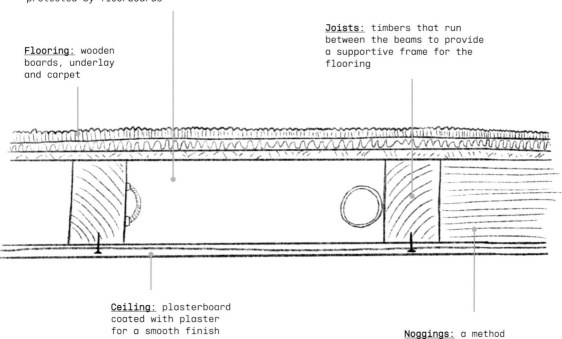

Ceiling: plasterboard coated with plaster for a smooth finish

Noggings: a method of bracing timbers to prevent them bowing under weight

Ceilings

Ceilings are essentially the underside of the floor above, but this doesn't mean they have be boring. You may want them to be anonymous – but you may not! Most ceilings have a layer of plaster over the top of plasterboard to create a smooth and even finish. If you have hanging ceiling lights that draw the eye upwards, why not make a feature of them with a few decorative touches? You will also need to hide any unsightly features, such as ceiling and wall joins or cracks.

ARTEX

Who's he, then – does he play right back for Arsenal? The name may not be familiar but you would recognize Artex straight away if you saw it. It's a decorative surface coating that you'll often find on ceilings, which was most popular in the 1970s. It looks like plaster but is a much simpler to apply and anybody can do it. It creates a textured finish: stipples and swirls are really popular designs.

It can be a right pain, though. If you've inherited an Artex ceiling that's looking a bit worse for wear, the bad news is that you can't repair it, as it's almost impossible to recreate the pattern. And there's worse news: until 1984, Artex was made using asbestos, so if you want to get rid of it you need to get it checked out professionally. If there's asbestos there, you'll have to pay a licensed contractor to remove it.

CEILING TILES

You normally find these in offices as a cheap, easy-to-fit ceiling finish, but some home owners use them, too. They're normally made from polystyrene, but more stylish mineral-fibre versions are getting more popular now.

Ceiling tiles can simply be glued to the ceiling as you would fit ordinary tiles. Some come in tongue and groove so they can be slotted together to create a continuous finish. Mineral-finish tiles require a little more effort, in that they need to be stapled to wooden battens secured to the ceiling first.

Oh, and a warning: don't use polystyrene tiles in a kitchen or any area that comes into contact with direct heat, such as around a fireplace.

MOULDINGS

Cornices run around the top of the walls to finish them off and hide any ugly joins between wall and ceiling. Think of them as a skirting board at the top of the wall! They're usually made of wood or plaster and can be glued or nailed into place. You can go for a simple curved design or something a bit fancier, if that's your thing. Your call!

LIGHT CENTREPIECE

If you have a central ceiling light, you might want to make an extra feature of it with decorative mouldings where the cable comes out of the ceiling.

Again, like cornices, there are usually made of wood or plaster and can be glued into place. They are mostly pretty lightweight, but if it's a large, heavy statement piece, you can also add some screws to secure it to the joists above – you don't want it falling on someone's bonce!

Basic Techniques

I've always said that DIY is all about common sense, using your tools correctly and using your noddle before you make any cuts or holes. There are some jobs that I'd advise you to seek professional help with, such as hanging doors or anything involving gas or electrics, because experience has taught me that although a job might look easy, it's sometimes way more difficult to get right than you imagine. And you need to stay safe – in the UK it is illegal to adapt your own electrics unless you are a qualified electrician, and the same goes for anything to do with gas.

SAFETY FIRST!

When it comes to DIY, it's crucial to take all the necessary safety precautions. Get this for a warning: on average, British hospitals treat around 300 patients a week who have been injured in DIY accidents!

During the 2020–21 Covid lockdown, with everyone in the UK stuck at home and wanting to fill the long hours, home improvements boomed, and so did related hospital admissions. More than 5,600 people were injured using power tools, 2,700 with non-powered hand tools, and eye injuries increased massively because DIYers didn't protect themselves properly.

So, here's a list of important considerations before you get started:

1 **Make sure the area you're working in is clear and organized.** It should have everything you need to hand and no trip hazards such as cables or piles of clutter.

2 **If you're working inside, make sure the room is well ventilated.** This is particularly important if you're using chemicals, strong-smelling paints or varnishes or doing any sanding.

3 **Use ladders with care!** Make sure they are properly opened and secured and set up on a stable, level surface before you use them. If you are using ladders higher than a stepladder, ask someone to hold them for you.

4 **Wear the right kit!** When sanding, blowtorching, cutting wood with power tools or using spray paint, wear a dust mask, gloves and safety goggles to protect your eyes against flying fragments.

5 **If you suspect old paint might be lead-based,** or your ceiling might contain asbestos, get advice from a qualified person before removing it and find out how best to dispose of it.

6 **Take great care when using tools:**
- Unplug power tools when you are not using them and make sure any blades are carefully stored and turned away from you.
- Always cut away from you when using a saw or knife.
- Keep tools sharpened and in good condition – sharp blades are safer than blunt ones.
- When using power tools, make sure all cables are secured.
- In any doubt? Call in a professional! Always get hold of a qualified electrician or certified gas engineer when dealing with electrics or gas. These jobs need specialist expertise and professional certification. Similarly, call a plumber for any jobs beyond fixing drips and clearing blocked U-bends. Believe me: you do not want water damage in your life!

CUTTING TILES

When you are laying tiles, it is easiest to start with laying the whole tiles. However, there are always sections at the edges, or around pipes in bathrooms or switches in kitchens, that need fiddly cutting to fit.

How do you cut these tiles? It depends on the type of tile you are using. Thinner ceramic tiles (about 15mm thick or less) can be cut easily using a tile scorer, if you are just cutting a straight line. Mosaic tiles can be cut with a Stanley knife. Thicker tiles might need a more heavy-duty solution such as hiring a tile-cutter machine. Mark on the tile with a pencil the section you need to cut. If you're cutting with a tile-scorer, hold a metal ruler along the line you have marked and score the line several times. Then place the pencil under the tile, along the line, and press down on each side of the tile to cleanly split it.

If you are cutting a curve from a tile, use a tile nipper or a hacksaw with a special blade. If the curve is particularly fiddly, create a template out of paper first to get it absolutely right, then place this on top of the tile and mark out the shape with a pencil. You can then score away a section of the tile, tidying up to the line with a tile nipper, or use the hacksaw to cut along the line.

SCRIBING WORKTOPS: BLOCK AND PENCIL METHOD

This works well if you have got a very uneven wall. Place the worktop against the wall and measure the widest part of the gap. Cut a small block of wood to this length. Place the block at one end of the worktop, against the wall. Put the tip of a pencil onto the worktop at the edge of the block. Holding it in place against the block, but still touching the worktop, slowly move the block along the wall, so that the pencil traces the outline of the wall. Use a jigsaw to saw along the pencil line.

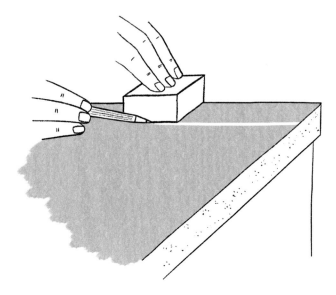

SCRIBING WORKTOPS: FREEHAND METHOD

Unless you're really lucky, the wall of your kitchen will be slightly uneven. This means that when you push your worktop into position against it, there will be some gaps. Don't panic! Scribing is a simple way of creating a neater finish, and it can be used on cabinets, mouldings and any other fixing that needs to sit against a wall.

For a worktop, push it against the wall and fix a piece of masking tape along it, with the tape edge running along the length of the worktop edge. With a pencil, mark the contours of the wall along the tape. Using a belt sander, sand along the line, then keep slotting the worktop against the wall and sand again until you get the perfect fit. Job's a good 'un!

SAWING CURVES

Not all cuts are straight, sadly. Or, are you looking to add a bit of interest to a room by introducing some curved lines? Either way, the best way to cut curves neatly in a piece of wood is using a jigsaw. And here's how you do it.

Mark up your desired curve, either freehand or using a template, then cut along the line using an electric jigsaw. Jigsaw blades are relatively thin, which make cutting a curve achievable, but it takes practice to get a smooth line. For that reason, I'd always advise having a practise go on some waste wood first and using a new, sharp blade. If your curved line ends up a bit wobbly, don't worry – sand it down to smooth out any bumps. The thinner the material you're cutting, the sharper you can make the curve.

SANDING

Now, sanding is absolutely fundamental to most DIY projects – but which sandpaper do you use? How many sheets will you need? And what the heck is a sanding block?

Let me explain! Sandpaper comes in varying levels of abrasiveness. This is called the 'grit', and it's measured using a numbering system. The lower the number, the coarser and rougher the sandpaper will be.

All sandpaper scratches the surface of whatever it's rubbed against. The coarser the sandpaper, the deeper those scratches will be. If you need to sand the edge of some sawn wood, for example, you might start off with a medium-to-coarse sandpaper to take off any really rough bits, but move on to a medium-to-fine sandpaper to give a smoother finish. Sandpaper sheets will last for multiple small jobs, especially if you fold them into a wad and keep changing the fold to use a different part of the paper.

If you need to achieve a flat surface, this is where a sanding block comes in. It is exactly what it sounds like: a block of wood, or other fairly solid substance, with perfectly flat surfaces that you can wrap sandpaper around.

STRIPPING WALLPAPER

If you want to freshen up your walls with new wallpaper or simply get rid of some sad-looking strips, you need to remove all of the paper completely first to create smooth walls for papering or painting.

There are a couple of options for how best to go about it. A simple solution of hot water with liquid detergent is about as eco-friendly as it gets, and cheap too! Apply this to the wallpaper surface to wet it and let it seep through to the back of the paper. A sponge or a spray bottle are best for this.

Another option is to steam the paper away by hiring power steamers. You just fill the tank with water, plug it in and hold the hot steam plate against the wallpaper. The steam will moisten the adhesive and make paper removal much easier. If you gently score the wallpaper first – taking care not to mark the wall underneath – it will help the water or steam to get behind the paper, enabling it to be gently lifted off.

Once the paper begins to loosen, you need to encourage it off the wall using a scraper or stripping knife to lift away the paper. This can get really messy as soggy paper falls away, so make sure you've protected the floor first!

If your wallpaper is particularly stubborn, you can buy chemical wallpaper-stripper that you spray or brush over the wallpaper. This will quickly dissolve the adhesive, making even the toughest removal jobs easier.

REMOVING PAINT

Sometimes, you can paint over existing paintwork as a short-term fix. However, there comes a point when the paint underneath is so old it is chipped, peeling or bubbling, which makes the new layer of paint look pretty scruffy – if it holds in the first place! When it gets to this point, you have no choice but to strip away the layers of old paint.

First, prepare the area as you would for paper-stripping. If you prefer to avoid chemicals, you can use a heat torch which you can buy or hire, but take care not to scorch the surface you're stripping. There are a lot of different paint strippers available on the market, so pick the one that best suits your needs – different ones are designed specifically for walls, timber frames and furniture, and some are more environmentally friendly than others, with fewer chemicals. If you are removing a lot of layers of paint, you may need a more heavy-duty stripper.

Brush the stripper onto the paint you want to remove. Leave it to do its magic for as long as the instructions on the packaging tell you. Once the stripper has softened and dissolved the paint, scrape away at a section of bubbling paint with your scraper and peel it off. Keep going until you've removed as much paint as possible. Once the flaked paint is cleared away, sand the surface to remove any last bits of paint.

Recycling, Reusing & Repurposing

I'll warn you now, and I make no apologies for it: we're going to talk a lot about recycling, reusing and repurposing in this book. And so we should! It's a great way to get the most out of what you have, save yourself some money and do your bit to look after the planet.

When you are giving your home a new look, don't forget that you don't have to buy everything new. See what you have, and think whether it can be repurposed to meet your needs and your new design scheme.

There are so many ways to do this! Old cupboards and drawers can be repainted or have new handles put on them to give them a fresh and updated style. Chairs that are looking a bit battered can be repainted or reupholstered with new stuffing and a fresh fabric. Old sofas don't have to hit the scrap heap; if the basic frame is still OK, buy or make new fitted or loose covers, or add more filling to sagging cushions.

If you're short of furniture – remember you don't have to choose expensive pieces! You can find really great bits at auctions or markets, in charity shops and at car-boot sales that can be in great nick or just need a little bit of attention to revitalize them.

It's a bit of a mission for me and it can be for you, too. One person's junk can be someone else's treasure. All that you need is a little bit of imagination, and the DIY skills that this book is about to teach you! Happy days!

Kitchen

Back in the day, when I was a kid, kitchens used to be pretty small and functional. In my family, it was just a room where my mum cooked.

The kitchen is where people let their inhibitions go and reveal their inner secrets. They put the kettle on and break the big news: 'Mum, guess what! I'm getting married!' It was the room where I first got told that I was going to be a dad. I don't know why, but you always seem to get the big life surprises in the kitchen!

Back in the day, when I was a kid, kitchens used to be pretty small and functional. In my family it was just the room where Mum cooked. You'd have a lino floor, ugly old cupboards and a freestanding cooker with a grill at the top. No such thing as extractor fans back then: opening a window and flapping a tea towel around was the only option when you burnt your toast.

Thankfully, the world has changed for the better, and so have kitchens. It's not just Mum who cooks now, we all have a bash, and kitchens aren't just poky, practical little spaces but beautiful, expansive rooms where the family can get together to dine, drink, chill out and, yeah, share those big secrets.

Everyone has their own preferences for what their kitchens should look like. Mine are very specific. I don't even want my kitchen to look like a kitchen: I want it to look like a gallery. An art gallery. I like my own kitchen to be really cool, with absolutely, definitely no clutter.

I like everything neat and tidy, with sleek, clean surfaces and proper moody lighting – probably just the one light bulb. You will never see knives and forks scattered around in my gaff, or saucepans hanging on the wall! The most you might see is a glass kettle for me to make my ginger tea with.

I don't mind having stuff out that you can just casually pick up and eat as you walk past, like fruit and nuts, but otherwise everything is tucked away where it needs to be. If I have the luxury of a big kitchen, I like to keep all utensils hidden. That's just me, and the way I am.

When I am at home, eating and music are my two favourite pastimes, so I make sure that the kitchen is well set up for both of them. And it's crucial to have somewhere to sit and chat, whether it's a conventional kitchen table and chairs, or bar stools and a breakfast bar.

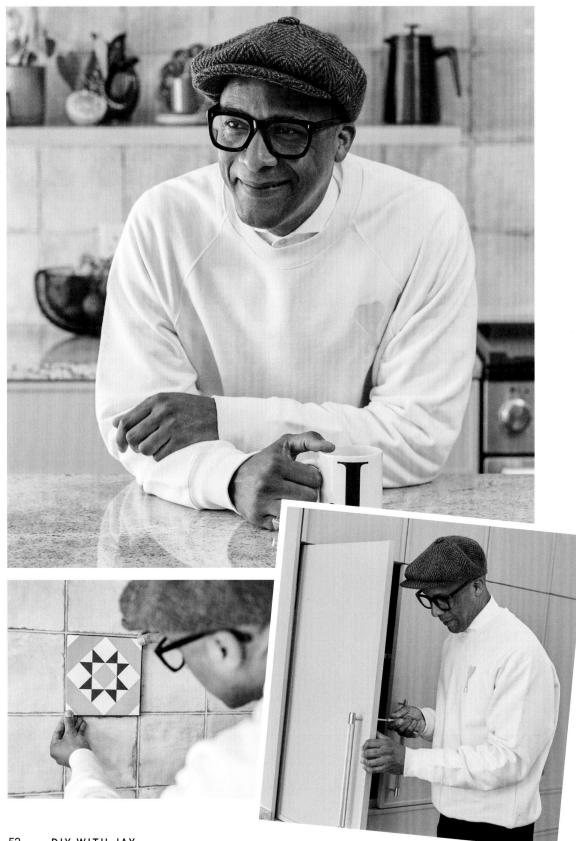

I'll teach you some tricks from my own specialist subject of reupholstering old chairs and giving them a new lease of life.

My ex-wife Jade and I made our own kitchen from scratch (a lot more about that later in this chapter) and there is no reason why you can't do the same thing. Seeing it come together before your eyes is the most rewarding and exciting process and will give you a real thrill. Trust me!

At the same time, there are so many kitchen features to think about before you start work. What kind of flooring do you want – real wood, laminate, vinyl or tiles? Do you want to renovate your existing cupboards, or get adventurous and install new ones to your own design?

When it comes to shelving, do you just want practical storage shelves or something a little more attention-grabbing and imaginative (I was going to say off-the-wall, but that's not quite right for shelves!). There's nothing wrong with either option, and I'll give you a few tips for both.

Worktops and sinks are crucial elements for any kitchen. What type of surfaces are you looking to feature and how can you make the most of them? If you're going to install your own sink, how do you make sure it is safe and watertight, and that you're not going to leave yourself needing a snorkel and flippers when you come to make a cup of Rosy Lee?

Your choice of tables and chairs will also define your space. Good news: you don't need to traipse down to a certain well-known Scandinavian supplier of self-assembly household furniture. I'll teach you some tricks from my own specialist subject of reupholstering old chairs and giving them a new lease of life.

Ultimately, as with any room in the house, what kind of kitchen you are looking for comes down to your personal taste and your individual needs. Do you need worktop space for a bread maker, a fancy coffee machine, slow cooker or microwave? What do you like cooking: do you need an area to make pasta, or decorate cakes?

And that's the key, my friends – think about what you most like to do in your kitchen, and what your ideal décor is, then plan accordingly. So, let's get cracking on the most important room in the home, so you can turn it into the perfect place to share those big life secrets . . .

Planning *your* kitchen

If you're doing a total kitchen overhaul, first of all, good luck to you! It's a major task, but don't be intimidated. With the right preparation and materials, you will be able to do a blinding job, then you'll look around and be proud of the results every single time you make a cuppa. Believe me!

As with every refit or DIY job, planning is crucial. And that's especially so if you are incorporating existing materials of specific sizes (like the toughened glass shelves that Jade and I used in our kitchen – we weren't getting those cut to size!). It doesn't matter if your drawing skills are a bit ropey, so long as you can measure your space and your materials and jot down an accurate plan for what is going to go where, then you're in business.

One really helpful way to visualize things is to get a roll of masking tape and a tape measure, then mark out on your floor where the different elements of your kitchen will go. Obviously, this works best if you have a fairly empty room to start with and have already taken out some or all of your old units and furniture.

THINK PRACTICALLY

As any decent online kitchen-planning tool will tell you, it's best to zone things in a practical way, so that when it comes to using your kitchen, you don't get annoyed that the only place you can plug in your kettle is on the other side of the room to the tap and the storage for teabags and mugs. It makes sense to have clear worktop space next to your cooker so your ingredients are to hand as you stir your pan, and it's a good idea to have easy access to the sink from there too, so you don't have far to travel with a hot pan of cooked pasta or potatoes when you need to drain the water.

This all sounds like common sense, and it is, but it's easy to overlook those sorts of basic details when you're in the middle of the re-vamp, and then be left slapping your forehead at the end like Homer Simpson – d'oh!

When it comes to sinks and anywhere that's near the hob, for me you've got to have splashbacks. You can make your splashback the same colour as the wall, or you can use contrasting tiles, or glass, or even just paint the wall with varnish so that it can be wiped down and kept clean. You always want your kitchen to look fresh; what you don't want is some guest turning up, noticing a stain on your wall and joking, 'Oh, I see you had spag Bol last week? Looks like it was tasty!' The best practical advice I can give you is to make sure that everything can be wiped and cleaned easily. That way, if and when you make a bit of a mess, it doesn't matter.

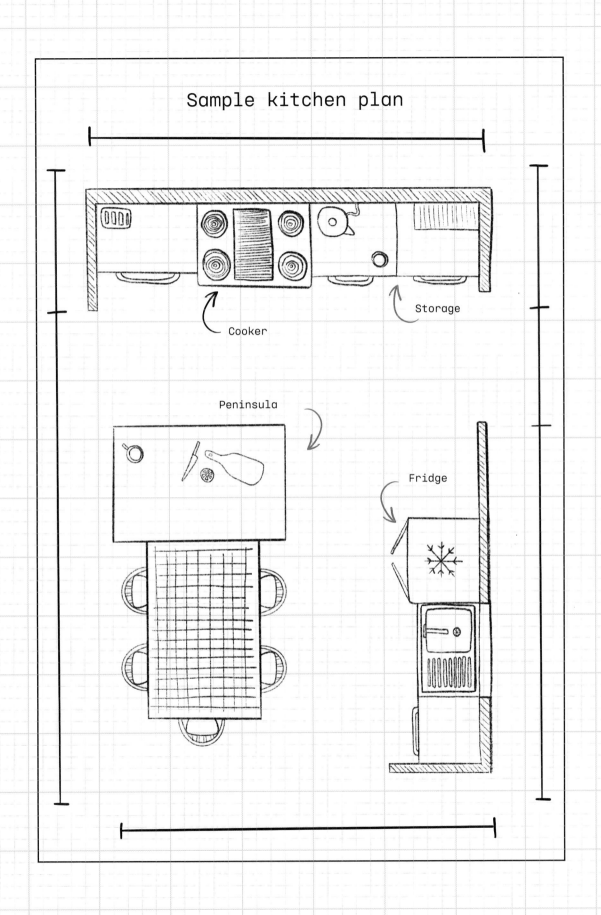

Sample kitchen plan

Cooker

Storage

Peninsula

Fridge

Kitchen Flooring

My favourite kind of flooring is something practical – and in a kitchen that means easily wipeable. In my first proper home we did the most cost-effective thing and painted the kitchen floor. It was one of the best things we did. We had loads of parties, with people spilling food, drinks and whatnot, or walking around in dirty shoes on it, and it was always easy to wipe down and get back to what it was. When the floor got a bit marked and chipped in places, we just painted it again! The floor was concrete, so we used a water-based gloss that dried in a couple of hours and meant the kitchen wasn't out of bounds for long.

You could do all sorts of other things, though. You can even lay down cork tiles, which would give you a nice warm feeling underfoot. Underfloor heating is great if you've got the money and don't mind the upheaval involved in fitting it but, if not, cork is cool (well, warm). Another cheap option is carpet tiles, but I would go for these only in certain areas and always away from the immediate food-prep spaces. Imagine red wine on a carpet tile? It's just not a good look!

PAINT IT

It's all well and good me telling you to slap some paint on your floor and – bosh! – job's a good 'un! But you do need to bear in mind that some flooring is easier to paint than others, and some types of paint will be more hardwearing than others. I'm hoping that I don't need to tell you clever people not to paint over a carpet!

WHAT CAN YOU PAINT?

- Wood
- Laminate with a real-wood surface
- Concrete
- Tiles

WHAT'S NOT ADVISABLE TO PAINT OVER?

- Vinyl flooring (*pull it up and you might be able to paint what's underneath*)
- Laminate with a plastic surface (*this might be OK if you sand it thoroughly. Test an out-of-sight section or offcut.*)
- Cork tiles
- Old tiles with a porous surface

›› Choosing paint

I used water-based gloss on my own floor, mainly because I hate the smell of oil-based gloss paint. Ideally you need to choose a paint that will stick to your floor the best and wear well, so you aren't touching-up the high-traffic areas every other week. Once you're clear what you are painting onto, you need to buy paint that's most suited to that surface. All paint tins will have instructions on how to prep the surface, and how long it will take to dry.

It's always worth buying a bit more than you think you'll need and returning any unopened cans. There are few things more frustrating than running out of paint midway through a job. Trust me – I've been there!

Jay's Top Tip

Sugar soap is a type of cleaner that's brilliant for degreasing. It is not a mixture of sugar and soap, despite the name!

›› Preparing to paint a kitchen floor

The most important thing is to make sure the existing floor is clean, dry and free from grease or oil. First and foremost, you need your paint to stick to the floor, and it won't if there are loose bits of old paint, toast crumbs or oily splodges about (you especially find these around ovens and hobs).

But before you do that, you'll need to get everything you can off the floor. Shift the dog bowls, the bins, the bag of recycling, any furniture and so on into another room (or out into the garden). Next, have a think about where you will start and finish painting. Ideally you need to start furthest away from the door and work yourself out of the room. Don't paint yourself into a corner, like Mr Bean!

Now get the vacuum into ALL the nooks and crannies, then give the floor a good wash with soapy water – or use sugar soap solution if there's any grease present. Take a good look at your floor. If there are any bits that need sanding down (for example, where there's loose paint, or old breakfast cereal that's welded itself to the surface) get those sorted. If you're painting over wooden laminate flooring, be sure to sand the surface well so that the paint will stick to it.

WOODEN FLOORBOARDS

If you're in an older property you might be lucky enough to have good old floorboards to work with. Even if there are areas that aren't looking so great, you might be able to patch in some reclaimed boards that look similar to your originals.

›› Stripping back to the wood

The key thing here is to use the most appropriate stripping method for whatever is on your boards, be that paint, varnish, or a mixture. You need to be careful with old gloss paint, though, as it may contain lead, and if it does, when you start stripping it the fumes can be really toxic. If you're in any doubt, buy a test kit and check a small section to find out for sure, and follow the guidelines you can find online for dealing with it.

THE MAIN WAYS OF STRIPPING PAINT ARE:

- <u>CHEMICAL:</u> use the most eco-friendly liquid stripper that you can find, and always follow the instructions properly.

- <u>HEAT:</u> heat gun or blow torch methods need to be handled with care, and are used in conjunction with a scraper to lift the heated paint. This isn't a practical option for large areas.

- <u>ABRASION:</u> sanding the paint or varnish off can work well but always wear a mask so you don't breathe in the dust. See below for more info.

SANDING AND SEALING

You'll need to hire a big belt or disc sander for the main floor area, and a smaller edging sander for the edges, and be sure to ask for spare sanding belts and discs too. Speak to your local hire shop to establish the best options for your floor. Again, you'll need to completely clear the room and it's important to prepare the floor as for painting, but in addition you will need to drive down all screws or nails that are already in the floor to 2–3mm below the surface to prevent damage to the sander. Once the floor is sanded smooth and you've vacuumed up every last bit of sawdust, apply your choice of finish (varnish, wax and oil are the most popular), following the manufacturer's instructions.

Jay's Top Tip

There are legal guidelines for dealing with old paint that contains lead. Find the latest online at hse.gov.uk and search for lead paint.

›› Filling gaps

Old floorboards often have small gaps in between them, and if these are big enough to lose coins through, or let draughts in, they need filling! You can buy flexible filler specifically for filling floorboard gaps. This is great if you have uneven gaps or funny shapes to deal with, such as around radiator pipes. You can also buy slivers of reclaimed pine floorboards to use as fillers for larger gaps – this is fiddlier but it gives the best finish. The easiest method if you have a lot of long, straight gaps to fill (and especially if you've already sanded and sealed the floor) is a kind of 'V' profile tape that comes on a roll. You just push it into the gap and it springs apart to fit the space.

LAMINATE & ENGINEERED WOOD

There are absolutely loads of options out there in this area, but they all work in the same way – you simply buy packs of standard-sized boards that slot together with a tongue-and-groove join at the sides and ends. The boards lock together (or are glued together) to create a 'floating floor' that doesn't need to be nailed, screwed or glued to the subfloor. It is important to leave an expansion gap around the edges – and this can be hidden under a trim that you glue or nail to your skirting boards, or by raising your skirting boards so that they hover very slightly above the surface of the floor, allowing for a little movement as the temperature changes and the floating floor expands and contracts.

Fitting this type of floor yourself is straightforward, as long as you have a fairly level sub-floor to start with. Whichever system you choose, look at the manufacturer's recommendations for underlay, and be sure to factor in the cost of this when you're making plans. For this type of flooring, you need to start laying it in one corner of your room, then work in rows until the whole floor is covered. You will probably need to cut a strip from the bottom of any doors to accomodate the new floor level.

Jay's
Top Tip

It's really important to acclimatize your boards – or any natural material – to the temperature and moisture levels in your home before you start to use them. Put them in the room they'll be used in for 48 hours before you start laying them.

❯❯ Preparing your subfloor

As with preparing to paint (see page 58), your floor needs to be clean, dry and free from any lumps and bumps. If you've taken up carpet or vinyl flooring, do take the time to remove any stray bits of adhesive or carpet tacks left behind. Look out for any floorboard nails or screws that might have loosened and are sticking up – hammer them down, screw them back in place or take them out altogether.

If your subfloor is level or just a little uneven, the underlay you use will create a level 'cushion' for your boards. If your subfloor is very uneven, you will need to lay sheets of hardboard or plywood first, before topping with the underlay. You should start in the middle of your floor and work outwards for this stage, cutting boards to fit around the sides of the room, and leaving an expansion gap at the very edges.

❯❯ Underlay

It's crucial to use underlay to provide insulation, shock absorption, soundproofing and a moisture barrier (if laying flooring on top of concrete) and to smooth out any tiny lumps and bumps, which will help to reduce wear on your floor surface. There are tons of types of underlay available, from spongy foam or cork that comes on a roll to wood-fibre panels. Look at what is recommended for use with your chosen flooring and the type of subfloor you have, then select the best option for your circumstances.

›› Is my floor flat?

There are a few ways to check this. First, take a careful look at it. If it looks a bit wonky, it probably is! If you have a long measuring stick or a plank of wood, turn it onto one of its long, thin edges and lay it across the floor. Do this in several places across your floor. Does it make contact with the surface all the way along? If so, your floor is even; if there are gaps here and there, it isn't flat.

NEW SOLID WOOD FLOORBOARDS

You can lay new (or reclaimed) boards on top of an existing wooden floor – or on top of a plywood subfloor. These can be nailed down as individual planks using the secret nailing technique.

Step *by* Step

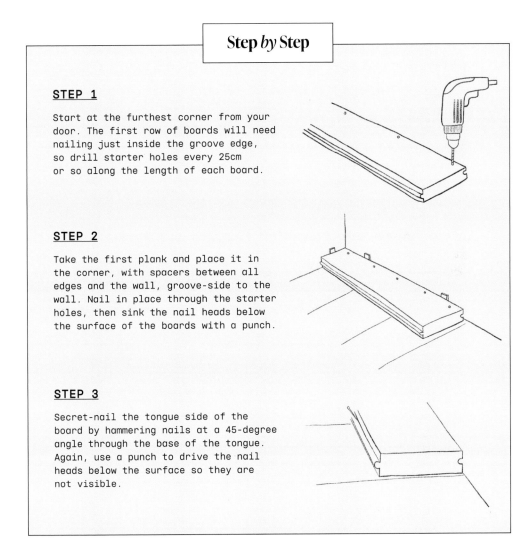

STEP 1

Start at the furthest corner from your door. The first row of boards will need nailing just inside the groove edge, so drill starter holes every 25cm or so along the length of each board.

STEP 2

Take the first plank and place it in the corner, with spacers between all edges and the wall, groove-side to the wall. Nail in place through the starter holes, then sink the nail heads below the surface of the boards with a punch.

STEP 3

Secret-nail the tongue side of the board by hammering nails at a 45-degree angle through the base of the tongue. Again, use a punch to drive the nail heads below the surface so they are not visible.

SOFT FLOOR TILES

Tiles for a kitchen floor are a practical choice – they are easy to clean and can look really smart. You can lay ceramic tiles in a kitchen, but personally I think they can feel a bit cold underfoot, and if you drop any china or glass I can pretty much guarantee it'll be in a thousand pieces as soon as it hits the floor! (See the bathrooms section for how to choose and install ceramic tiles.)

Vinyl or rubber floor tiles are a great option as they are easy to keep clean but are not as cold and hard as ceramic. I've already mentioned cork tiles – they're warmer underfoot, but you do need to seal them and potentially re-seal them every few years to keep them looking tip-top. Carpet tiles are very hard-wearing and can work well in areas of the kitchen less prone to spillages. Whichever you feel is right for you, all of these flexible tiles are laid in a similar way.

Jay's Top Tip

Don't assume that your floor is perfectly rectangular or square with 90-degree angles at its corners. Have a good butcher's and check everything first. It will prevent tears further down the line.

❯❯ Laying soft floor tiles

With any of these flexible types of tiles, you're basically going to glue them to your floor with whatever type of adhesive is recommended by the manufacturer – unless you're using self-adhesive tiles, in which case all you need to do is peel off the backing and stick them down onto your smooth, even, clean and dry subfloor. You'll need to work methodically, but it's not a difficult task if you get yourself organized.

In order for any joins between tiles or the pattern in your tiles to look straight, you need to first mark your floor with a central cross to show the up/down and right/left lines you'll follow. (See page 25 for how to snap a chalk line.)

Once you have your central cross, the usual method is to work from the centre out towards one wall, spreading adhesive for a few tiles at a time so that it doesn't dry before you have chance to lay them carefully on top. Make sure you have the right tools for cutting tiles to fit at the edges of the floor, or around radiator pipes or door frames.

There are situations where working from the centre outwards isn't the best method – such as with small spaces where you want to have whole tiles centered in a doorway as you enter a bathroom, for example. In that case simply adapt the method shown opposite, making sure your marked cross aligns with the top and side edges of the first tile.

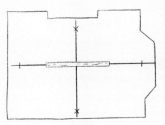

STEP 1

Mark your floor with a central cross, then nail down a guide batten along one of the lines.

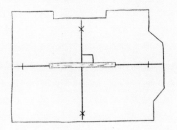

STEP 2

Spread adhesive, if using, in the first quadrant above the batten, or peel the backing off a tile, then lay the first tile carefully with the batten and line as a guide.

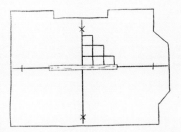

STEP 3

Repeat for the second tile, again being really careful to line it up with the previous one and the batten perfectly.

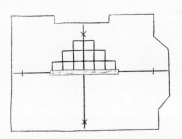

STEP 4

Continue laying tiles along the batten at first, but also moving upwards in a pyramid shape.

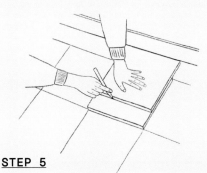

STEP 5

When you get to the edges of the room, cut perfect margin tiles by laying two loose tiles on top of the one it will butt up to. Carefully slide the top tile only to meet the wall. Draw along the edge onto the loose tile underneath.

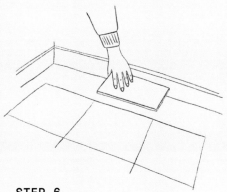

STEP 6

Cut along the mark and the piece of tile should fit the gap.

Cupboards

Kitchen cupboards are an essential part of any kitchen – for me, they enable you to have a sleek, clutter-free look to your room while still having all the plates, pots, glasses and so on to hand. Back in the place I lived in for years, we built our own lower cupboards by using bricks to create solid walls for their sides, then we fitted rustic-style farmhouse doors at the front. It was cheap, simple if you have some bricklaying skills (my years working the building sites came in well handy) and really, really solid!

Of course, you could also buy new or second-hand kitchen units and install them according to the manufacturer's instructions. But if you think about it, a cupboard is just a big square or rectangular frame with a door on the front. Got a solid old chest of drawers? Take the drawers out and there's your cupboard frame! You can even use the drawer runners to fix shelves to.

TRADITIONAL UNITS

Kitchens take a lot of wear and tear. It's important that all of your cupboards are solid and strong, so make sure that what you're buying or repurposing is well made and will stand the test of time. If you are building your own flatpack cupboards, it's advisable to put some wood glue onto the wooden dowels before locating them and to make sure that all of the screws are tightened up properly.

For wall units, it's really important that you use the right screws for your wall – see pages 30–31 for more details on this. As with any DIY job, measure twice and make sure that your marks for where to drill any holes are level.

JAY-STYLE BRICK CUPBOARDS

If you want to take a leaf out of my book and build the ultimate in solid base cupboards, good old bricks and mortar are your friends here . . . IF your kitchen has a solid floor, such as concrete. Don't build brick divider walls in a converted flat with springy floorboards. You do need to plan carefully, and remember to take into account the width of your bricks, especially if you have doors of a specific width, or appliances that you need to fit in between the walls.

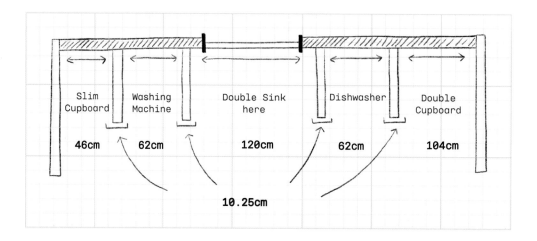

CUPBOARD DOORS

There are loads of options when it comes to doors, and when you think about it, a door is just a piece of timber, glass, metal or solid composite material that fits over an opening and has hinges down one side. If you are buying kitchen units the chances are that there will be a variety of door options depending on the look you're going for and your budget. These options will all come with hinges and closures that work with the units, which makes life pretty straightforward.

And what if you want to be a bit different? You can get really creative here, but do remember a few basic things:

- Don't put heavy doors on flimsy units.
- Be careful what you put in steamy areas: untreated timber above a kettle, for instance, could swell and warp.
- Wipe-clean surfaces are always the most practical in a kitchen.

The way I made my cupboard doors back in the day was by a very traditional door-making method using planks.

I measured the space, cut lengths of tongue-and-groove cladding to the correct height, then slotted the right number of pieces together for the width. Once I was sure my 'door' was the right size, I nailed everything to a 'Z'-shaped ledges-and-brace backing made of plain timber.

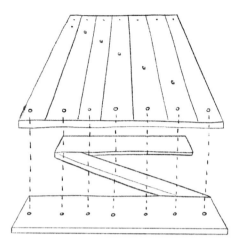

Jay's Top Tip

The worktop will need to be level, and your floor might not be. You might have to make adjustments to any kitchen unit 'feet' or to build or cut frames to account for a sloping floor.

›› Hinges

Standard kitchen units come with hinges that look quite complicated, but if you read the instructions it should be clear that you can turn various different bits with a screwdriver to alter the alignment of the door. This is great if you are installing a bank of wall cupboards, for example, and you want the gaps between the doors to be perfectly even. However, if you're adopting a non-standard approach, you will need to choose the style of hinge that suits your overall look. Do you want them on show? Do you want them hidden? Are you going for a rustic farmhouse look or something sleeker and more engineered?

When it comes to fitting hinges, take your time to get the alignment perfect. If you're fitting them with no pre-drilled holes in the door or frame, fix the hinges to the door first, then take your time to mark the frame in exactly the right position. Drill holes for the bottom screw of each hinge into the frame using a drill bit that's a size smaller than your screws, then screw in the bottom screw on each hinge only, to check the alignment. If it isn't quite right, make the necessary adjustments, re-mark, drill, screw – and repeat.

Shelves

Shelves are such a simple and effective form of storage, but in a kitchen I'd strongly advise using a material that you can really easily wipe to remove any muck. Back in my old house we had toughened glass shelves that came from an old shop-fitters company, and they were so simple to clean. If you do want to use timber, or any board that is porous, I'd recommend painting it with water-based gloss paint, or using vinyl wrap to cover them. This applies to shelves inside a cupboard, too – they can still get things spilt on them or marks from the bottoms of saucepans, so my mantra for the kitchen is always to make everything wipeable.

The shelves obviously need to be level, as well! I can't say this enough: measure twice, and always use a level. Your floor or ceiling may not be perfectly horizontal.

WALL-HUNG SHELVES

Once you've decided what you'll use as a shelf, you need a way to fix it to your wall. Shelf brackets are the most popular way of doing this, and there is a huge range available. These usually come in an 'L' shape or similar, and are either screwed to the wall below the shelf or above it, depending on the design. It's crucial that the brackets are appropriate for the size and weight of your actual shelf and what you intend to put on it: a heavy piece of timber isn't going to stay up long if it is supported by flimsy brackets intended for a tiny, lightweight piece of MDF. See pages 30–31 for details on choosing the right screws and wall plugs for your type of wall.

ALCOVE SHELVES

If you've got any sort of alcove in your kitchen, such as next to an old chimney breast, this is an ideal place to put shelves as you can easily create 'floating' shelves, which look great and don't need traditional brackets. What you will need is a shelf that is cut to the exact width of the alcove and some wooden battens.

Jay's Top Tip

Make your shelves flush with the wall at the back so little things can't get trapped or lost behind them. If your wall is uneven, you can use filler to close any small gaps.

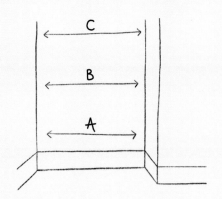

STEP 1

Measure the width of the alcove at the exact height you want to put each shelf – this might not be exactly even all the way down the wall space if your walls aren't perfectly straight. Cut the shelves to fit and mark lightly in pencil which shelf goes where if the widths vary a little. Cut a long piece of batten to the same length as the back of each shelf.

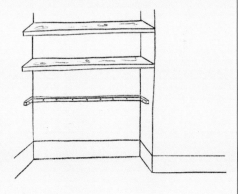

STEP 2

Measure the depth of the shelves and cut two pieces of batten for each shelf that are approximately two-thirds of this measurement. Cut one end of each batten at a 45-degree angle.

STEP 3

Drill two holes in each piece of side batten and four to eight in the batten for the back. Mark the wall with the positions of the holes and drill accordingly. The angled end of the side battens should be at the front, with the longest edge uppermost. Attach the battens to the wall: be sure to use the correct screws and wall plugs.

STEP 4

Slot the shelf into the alcove on top of the battens, then secure it in place with small wood screws on the back and sides.

A kitchen shelf is usually practical, but that doesn't mean you can't get well inventive. In one kitchen, I got a big fallen branch from a tree, brought it home and got it all dried out. Then I drilled holes through it and screwed it to the wall for a nice earthy, natural feature that served as a little shelf. It wasn't a practical shelf that you could put glass and other heavy bits and bobs on, it was more of a decorative feature, but my little daughter Zola used to keep a stuffed fabric bird on the branch, and we could easily hang things from it – and it looked brilliant, too!

I think that is a great example of something to keep in mind when you are revamping your kitchen or, indeed, anywhere in the house. Put your own mark on the gaff, dare to be different – and don't ever be afraid to think outside the box.

Worktops

A kitchen isn't a kitchen without space to prepare and serve out food – and worktops are the universal answer to that need. You can buy a vast range of different worktops, but you could also make your own by cutting any kind of durable board to size. What you always need to bear in mind is that – guess what? – worktops tend to get wet, so whatever you decide to use, the finish must be waterproof.

FITTING WORKTOPS

Worktops that fit against a wall will always be supported at the back by a wooden batten fixed to the wall at the right height. It's crucial that you measure carefully and install the batten so that it is level, making a back rail for your worktop to sit on top of. Small, metal L-shaped brackets are usually secured on the underside of the worktop to fix it to the batten. The front part of the worktop will usually be supported by the cupboards underneath, but if your kitchen includes a big section of worktop with a void underneath, you may also need to use a prop or props at intervals to make sure it doesn't start to bow.

Any small gaps at the back of your worktop where your wall isn't straight will be covered up by a thick-enough splashback, but if your wall is very wonky you might need to cut the back of the worktop to the right shape using the scribing technique (see pages 44–45).

CUTTING HOLES

If you are installing a sink it should come with a template that you use to make the correct-sized hole in your worktop for it to fit into. If you are reusing an old sink, you can make your own template by tracing round the hole in the previous worktop onto a big sheet of paper (lining paper or a roll of brown paper is often big enough). If you are creating your own template from the sink itself, remember that you need a hole smaller than the outer edge of the sink so that there is a lip all around for it to rest on. This is usually about 12mm, but check the manufacturer's website for details. Always err on the side of 'smaller' for the hole – you can cut more out, but you can't put it back!

STEP 1

Place your template in the correct position on your worktop piece, but ensure you have equal space at the front and back of it for the greatest stability. Mark the worktop carefully for where you will cut, then check it once you've finished.

STEP 2

Drill holes at the corners on the inside edge of the line, on the part that will be discarded. They need to be big enough for your electric saw blade to fit into.

STEP 3

Ensure you are using a sharp, new blade that makes its cut on the downstroke so that the surface of the worktop won't be chipped. If you're unsure, test an offcut first. Cut along your marked line slowly and carefully, making sure the central part that is being cut out is properly supported as you work.

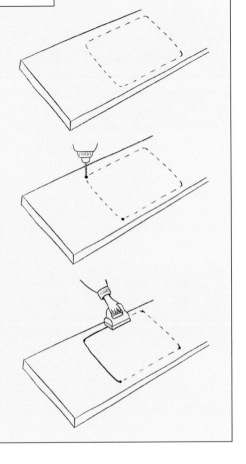

TILING WORKTOPS

Ceramic tiles are a great choice for kitchen worktops – they are heatproof, waterproof and very hardwearing. Marine plywood makes an ideal base surface, and you can install this as you would any other type of worktop. Always start tiling at the front edge, so that any tiles that are cut to fit will be at the back. (See pages 162–168 for more detail on tiling.)

Jay's Top Tip

Make sure the area being tiled is clear of any small tools! This is especially important if you are installing mosaic tiles that come on a big flexible sheet. When Jade and I tiled our kitchen, we ended up with a suspicious lump in one of our kitchen worktops – and, at the same time, my favourite small screwdriver disappeared. We kept the 'hill' under the mosaic tiles as a worktop feature because it made us laugh, but I do miss that screwdriver!

Splashbacks

For me these are absolutely essential in any kitchen. Face it, it's gonna get messy in there sometimes, so you need to be able to clean up properly and not leave tomato sauce or curry stains on your paintwork. You can use anything that's wipeable as a splashback. If you visit any DIY store they will have a load of splashbacks made from a range of materials. You can simply buy one of these off-the-peg solutions or do something a bit more bespoke, depending on the amount of time you have available and your budget. If you're really short on time and money you could even just varnish your wall at the back of the worktops; it's not the best solution but at least it saves you from gravy-stain grimness.

TILED SPLASHBACKS

Tiles work really well as splashbacks, and they are easy to install yourself. You can very simply vary the splashback height for different areas of your kitchen, plus it's a great way of masking wonky walls. If you've got lots of different elements to tile around, mosaic tiles can really be your friend here – but whatever you choose to use, make sure you've got the right tile-cutter for your tiles, and that you measure and plan well so you can buy the correct amount. (See page 163 for more about tiling walls.)

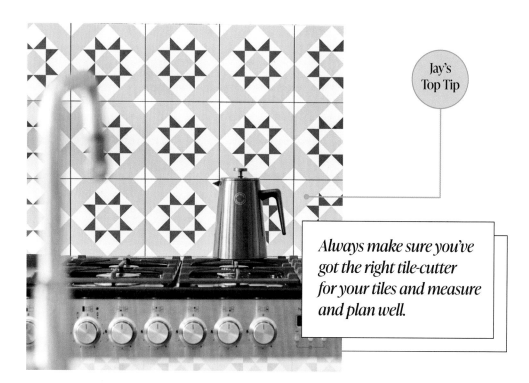

Jay's
Top Tip

Always make sure you've got the right tile-cutter for your tiles and measure and plan well.

GLASS

A lot of people use glass nowadays because it is easy to wipe down. Nothing really sticks to it and you can also have something behind the glass to give some colour, or use coloured glass. There are lots of companies that will make a splashback to your measurements, even giving you cut-out holes for sockets. Alternatively, you can buy tempered glass panels in standard sizes. All these options are easy to install yourself so long as your wall is fairly flat, without pipes, sockets or fuse panels in the way.

It's a great creative idea to add a bit of light to glass splashbacks. If you buy a strip of little LEDs, you can put them on the top, behind or, even better, the bottom edge of the splashback panel to give it a fabulous glow. Even cooler is if you buy LEDs with the option of different colours, all controlled with a little remote control. It's cushty! Just push a button and watch your kitchen wall flashing away! Here's my own special way of lighting up a kitchen splashback with LEDS.

Step *by* Step

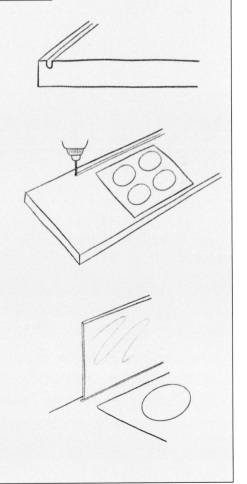

STEP 1

Use a router to cut a small channel at the back of your worktop, big enough for the LED strip to fit into. If you don't have a router, you can get this done at big hardware stores before you install the worktop. It's best to do this on timber surfaces but it is possible on other materials – check before you buy.

STEP 2

Insert the LED strip into the channel, after the worktop has been fitted. For a neat finish, drill through the worktop where the splashback will end so that the wire for the lights can be below the surface, plugged in out of sight.

STEP 3

Install the glass splashback according to the manufacturer's instructions, so that the bottom aligns with the strip of LEDs. Switch on and admire your work!

The Kitchen Sink & Friends

If you're using your kitchen, you'll be spending time at the sink washing stuff, whether it's pots and dishes (even if you've got a dishwasher, there are always some things you can't put in), fruit and veg, or just your hands. If it's practical, it is always best to have your sink in front of a window. It's not just a question of having a nice view to look at – it also means you can actually see what you're doing when you've got a bit of daylight!

TYPES OF SINK

When it comes down to it, all sinks are basically waterproof bowls with a drain at the bottom, connected to a waste pipe that flows into the outside drain. There's usually an overflow drain, somewhere near the top of the sink, that makes it impossible to leave a tap running and flood your kitchen. These also connect into the main waste pipe via a smaller pipe, and they are a godsend for the more forgetful among us.

Many modern sinks have an edge or lip that sits on top of your work surface, which are then secured underneath with clips and/or screws. If you're buying a new sink, these often come with a template for you to cut the right size and shape of hole out of your worktop. (See the worktops section on pages 72–73 for more detail on this.) The exception to this is Belfast sinks, or butler sinks as they are also known. These have no lipped edge, so they have to sit below the top of your work surface. However, the same principle applies when it comes to cutting out the correct-sized hole from your worktop – take accurate measurements!

» Sealant

Water has a nasty habit of dripping and splashing further than you might think. The problem is that if it gets into any type of wood it can cause it to swell and warp. So, it's important to seal around the edge of your sink with a proper mastic sealant. This is a doddle to do as long as you follow some basic guidelines. (See page 177 for more details.)

Jay's Top Tip

For any screw-together pipework, don't forget to wrap plumbers' tape (PTFE tape) around the bumpy thread end before screwing the other part on. This will form a watertight seal.

DISHWASHER AND WASHING MACHINE

These are usually made in fairly standard widths and depths but they can vary, so bear this in mind when planning your kitchen. Make double-sure you have the proper spec measurements for your machines and place them where it's easy to plumb in their pipes to the water supply and the waste pipes.

As the risk of stating the obvious, you will also need to plug in these appliances, so make sure you have plug sockets available nearby that comply with the latest safety regulations. Get a certified electrician to give them a once-over if you're in any doubt.

Here's one to ponder: do you want these kitchen appliances built in, with a cabinet door fixed onto them to make them a seamless part of your kitchen, or are happy to have them visible below a stretch of worktop? If it's the latter, you might want to look at options other than white. You can get washing machines or dishwashers in silver or even black to help give your kitchen a sleek, sexy look. And who wouldn't want a sexy kitchen?

PLUMBING FOR EVERYONE

We used to always leave plumbing to plumbers, but now there's more scope for some easy DIY. The beauty is that you don't have to use a blowtorch or need welding skills to do basic plumbing. There are some great push-fit systems that are really simple. You've got all the U bends, you've got the corners, all you do is push them together – and that's it! Job's a good 'un!

You do need to figure out how long the connecting pipes need to be, though, but with some measuring and common sense, this is straightforward. There are special pipe-cutting tools that make cutting pipes so easy, but a little hacksaw and a bit of elbow grease will do the job,

DIY home plumbing! It's the way forward! Having said that, it's always a good idea to get a professional to come around, check what you've done and sign it off. You can't be too safe – and assuming you've done a sensible and careful job, it'll still be a lot cheaper than paying them to do the whole lot.

Tables & Chairs

If you've got the space, it's really great to have some sort of seating in your kitchen, even if it's just a couple of bar stools pulled up to the worktop. Kitchens are sociable places! My ideal kitchen always has a table and chairs in it, and I especially love having a black table with really fun pops of colour from the plates and cutlery, and cups or glasses. I will often paint a table black, or just the legs, but another great thing you can use is the sticky-backed vinyl that comes on a roll – totally wipe-clean and very budget-friendly. If you've got wooden chairs that have seen better days, painting them is also a great option, as that way you are giving them a new life and can pick the colour (or colours) to work with your overall look at much less expense than buying new ones.

WALL-MOUNTED TABLE

You can buy these as a flatpack kit, but it's really easy to make your own with some fairly basic tools and materials. You'll need a piece of board for your tabletop that's a practical length for your space, two pieces of wooden batten that are long enough to support the length of your tabletop, leaving a gap in the middle for the folding bracket. Screws, hinges and a foldable bracket for the propping mechanism and you're laughing. Oh, and round off the table corners that will stick out – trust me, you don't want to be bashing into a sharp corner at table height!

Jay's
Top Tip

If you're short on space some folding chairs and a fold-down tabletop can work really well.

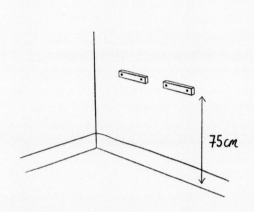

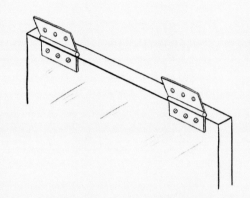

STEP 1

Attach the pieces of batten to your wall using appropriate screws and wall plugs. Standard tabletop height is 75cm or thereabouts.

STEP 2

Attach hinges to the underside of the wall edge of your tabletop.

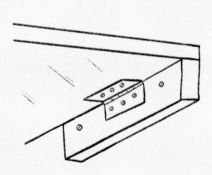

STEP 3

Attach the tabletop to the wall batten at the free side of each hinge. You may need someone to help hold it in place while you do this.

STEP 4

Hold the tabletop up so that it is level, then mark the wall where the screw holes for the folding bracket will go, drill into the wall, insert the wall plugs and screw the folding bracket in place.

THE RIGHT CHAIRS

There are so many different types of chair available, but you just need to choose ones that work for you. Do you want them to stack out of the way when not in use, or fold up and hang on the back of a door to give you more space? Would you prefer that they make a statement? Or do you need them to be sturdy enough that your kids can't tip over on them? What I would say is that it's worth buying chairs that are solidly made and can stand some wear and tear. Rather than buying new ones, can you get hold of better-quality chairs for the same price second-hand? Some of the most widely available second-hand chairs are the type with wooden backs and upholstered seats, and it's usually really simple to change the fabric to something that fits your décor. All you'll need is some replacement fabric, fabric shears and a staple gun or strong glue.

Jay's Top Tip

Take pictures of each stage of removing the old seat fabric to use as a reference when attaching the new fabric. This can be especially useful for getting the corners nice and neat.

Step *by* Step

STEP 1

Remove one of the drop-in seats by pushing up from the bottom. It should pop out easily.

STEP 2

Carefully remove the tacks or staples holding the fabric in place. Take the fabric off and smooth it out to reveal its shape.

STEP 3

Use the old fabric as a template to cut out the same-sized piece from your new fabric. If your material has a pattern, think about centring the main motif on each seat, or choosing a different aspect of the pattern for each individual seat.

STEP 4

With a seat centred on a new fabric piece, pull the back edge over and staple or glue it in place, leaving the corners free.

STEP 5

Carefully but firmly pull the fabric taut at the front and fold over to the underside of the chair. Staple or glue in place, again leaving the corners free.

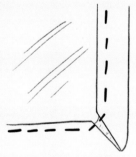

STEP 6

Repeat steps 4 and 5 for the sides. Pleat the fabric at each corner to give a neat finish and staple or glue in place. Trim off any excess fabric and replace the seat in the chair frame.

My Favourite...

KITCHEN TABLE AND CHAIRS

You spend so much time in the kitchen that you have to feel happy and relaxed when you are in there. One of the features I dreamed up that I am the proudest of was co-ordinating our artwork and our furniture.

Jade's brother, Imre, does a lot of drawing and painting. He's a proper talented artist. One time I saw that he'd drawn a huge picture based around four bright, vivid colours. My daughter Zola loved it, and I asked Imre, 'Can we have that, please?'

Imre gave it to us and I gave it pride of place in the kitchen. It looked blinding but I wanted to focus the room around it even more – which was when I had the idea of mirroring it in our kitchen furniture. A-ha!

I got hold of four old wooden wheelback chairs – those classic wooden chairs with wheel designs within their back spindles – and I painted one in each of the colours that Imre had utilized in his artwork: pink, blue, yellow and mauve. I took care to make them an exact match.

We had a black-topped kitchen table at the time, so I put it directly beneath Imre's painting and arranged the four multicolour chairs around it. Because of the blackness of the table, it drew out and emphasized all of the colours surrounding it, both in the artwork and the chairs.

It was such a simple idea. it was both subtle and striking, and it worked brilliantly – I spent even more time in the kitchen after that! So, there's a tip for you: think about colours that play off each other, and what you can do with them.

Living

Room

The only important thing about your home is that you love it and you feel happy and comfortable there.

Before I tell you what my ideal living room looks like, I want to make one thing clear: there are no rules. There is absolutely no reason why you should want to make your home look like mine or anybody else's.

In fact, I bet a lot of people wouldn't even like my gaff! I'll admit right now that my own recipe for the perfect living room is a little bit idiosyncratic. In the same way that I explained that I love my kitchen to look like an art gallery, I like my living room to have the basic aesthetic of a hotel room. I don't mean that I want it to be sterile and impersonal, it's more that I can't stand messiness. I abhor clutter, and I'm pretty sure that my instinct is down to growing up in Caribbean houses that were always full of stuff that was totally unnecessary.

That memory haunts me. I used to go to visit my auntie's house and every inch of her sideboards or shelves would be full of ornaments and little crocheted doilies and coasters. Even as a kid, I used to think, Man, why is this room so busy? Just give me the plain stuff!

So, my ideal living room is pretty minimal. It will only have three chairs in it. That is one each for my partner and me to sit on, and a third one just in case we have someone come over to see us. To be honest with you, I don't do a lot of entertaining!

I like to keep it simple, so if I have a long, open-plan room, I won't have much more in there than those three chairs, a sideboard and a sofa. I'll admit that I like a nice, big, self-indulgent sofa you can collapse into as if you're sinking into a welcoming, cosy bed. Ah, yes! Perfect!

You might be wondering, Oi! Jay! Where's the telly? It might surprise you that the answer is that there isn't one. Or, rather, there isn't a TV set fixed on the wall. My ideal television is a projector tucked into the ceiling that you don't even notice unless you're looking for it.

Too many living rooms are designed around the TV, with all of the chairs turned to face it as if it's a god. I'd rather have the seats facing each other, so the room is about family, conversation and companionship. It means television is an option, but it doesn't dominate the room. This might sound funny, coming from a bloke who's on the telly all the time, but I'm way more about music. Music makes a home feel inviting. I always have it

For me a living room should be smart, and ideally quite chic, but mostof all it needs to be the room that you long to come home to.

on. I've got my decks in my living room – at first glance, you'd think my old mate DJ Spoony or Fatboy Slim lived here!

Nor do I like to walk in and say, 'Alexa, play Bob Marley!' I can't be doing with that kind of technology. I like to physically put on a vinyl record. If I can get home, walk into my living room, smell food cooking in the kitchen and get my music going, that feels perfect to me.

The living room needs to be about comfort. If it has a solid floor, I like underfloor heating. Ideally, though, I want a soft, thick carpet. I know it's old school, and not fashionable, but I love a deep carpet that you can sink your feet into so that it feels like a quilt. Lovely stuff!

That's me, though! Like I say, your ideal living room may well be totally different, and I hope

this chapter can give you some ideas on how you might be able to achieve what you want. As with every other room in the house, you need to answer some basic questions before you get revamping.

Are you a fan of paint or wallpaper? Do you like a real fire or is that too much faff? What's your favourite colour scheme. (I love black, blue and yellow – I sussed out recently that they're the colours of the Barbadian flag! Must be a subconscious thing . . .) And what kind of lighting will put you firmly in full relaxation mode?

For me a living room should be smart, and ideally quite chic, but most of all it needs to be the room that you long to come home to, and chill out in, at the end of a busy day. So, let's make sure it is exactly that . . .

Planning *your* Living Room

The main problem with planning a revamp of your living space is that you're almost certainly already living in it! When it's full of your current furniture and décor, it can be hard to imagine how different it could look. So unless you can shift out all the stuff that's in it to make a blank space to size up, I'd grab good old-fashioned pencil and paper and get scribbling.

Take some measurements and make a plan of your room. Mark on the paper where the door is, the windows and any features in the room that you can't move, such as a fireplace. If you can, make a photocopy, so you can draw in the furniture as it is currently arranged on one plan, then compare it with your new ideas of what might go where.

You can even use coloured paper or card to represent your sofa, chairs, TV stand, sideboard or coffee table, and move them around on the main piece of paper to try different combinations. Don't do it near an open window, though, in case a sudden breeze wrecks your plans!

As well as this what-goes-where plan of the floor, you could apply the same logic to planning out each wall. I don't personally like to have much on my walls, but people who love to add decorative features, pictures or mirrors will find this exercise a big help.

THINK RELAXATION

What makes you feel relaxed and happy? Whatever it is, try to bring those elements into your living room. For me, smell is very important, and the good news is you don't need synthetic room spray to make your gaff smell lovely. Fresh flowers, a couple of cinnamon sticks or citrus peel in a bowl, or some scented candles – they can all add a natural and subtle scent to turn your house into a home.

Think about your other senses, too. Does music relax you, or do you like to come home to peace and quiet after a noisy day? What about touch – do soft, fluffy cushions ease your vibe, or do you prefer clean, sleek lines? Some people love seeing pictures of their family and friends while others – like me – love to chill out in a clutter-free space.

Have a good think about all this before you start planning. Your décor preferences will be unique to you, but if you can tune in to what really floats your boat, you'll be bang on track for creating a living room you love. Sorted!

PAINTING YOUR ROOM

First of all, move as much gear as you can out of the room you're going to be painting. If any stuff is too big, heavy or awkward to shift, cover it up with proper dust sheets that won't let paint through. You can use thick fabric drop-sheets that can be washed and reused – or, if you want to go down the disposable route, there are plenty of biodegradable options.

Next, get rid of those cobwebs, and anything else that might be lurking on your walls and ceiling that shouldn't be there! Stray picture hooks and nails are the usual culprits. Scrape off any loose and flaking paint, then sand down any rough or uneven parts so that your wall surface is smooth and even.

Finally, don't forget to protect your light switches, light fittings, doors and windows. Decorators' tape is best, because it's not too sticky and comes off easily without leaving a mark, but masking tape will also do the job.

Some ceiling roses can be unscrewed. This lets you paint the ceiling a little way under the rose to get the best finish. A handy hint: have you got complex, fiddly light fittings? Then stick compostable food-waste bags around them and tape them at the top to protect them while you paint.

Jay's Top Tip

Don't want to paint swatches of colour on your actual wall? Paint a piece of board instead, and move it round the room to see how it looks in the darkest corner and the lightest place.

›› Stripping wallpaper

Before you get all gung-ho and start taking wallpaper off your walls – hang on! Hold your horses!

Take a minute to think what might be underneath the paper. If you live in an old gaff, there's a chance the plaster underneath the wallpaper is in danger of crumbling – the paper may even be holding it together! Have a butcher's at your walls – are they a bit lumpy and bumpy? Maybe someone before you has literally papered over the cracks, in which case you'll have work to do once you strip it off.

But if you're confident that what lies beneath is solid and pukka, it's time to get that paper off. (See page 46 for more info on how to strip off old wallpaper without damaging the wall.)

›› Filling cracks

Thin, hairline cracks in your plasterwork? They're probably nothing to worry about, but if any are wide enough to fit a penny into, get the wall checked out by a professional to make sure you don't have any structural problems. Anything smaller, you can fill these in for a smoother look.

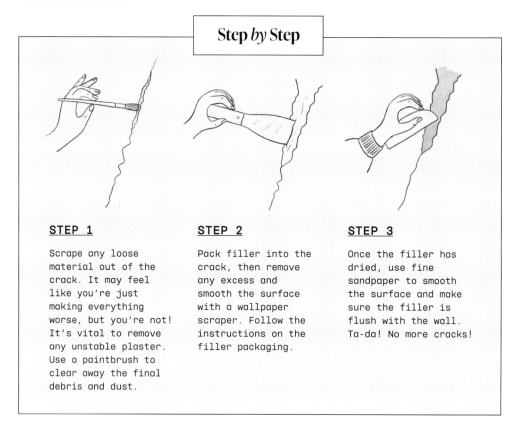

Step *by* Step

STEP 1

Scrape any loose material out of the crack. It may feel like you're just making everything worse, but you're not! It's vital to remove any unstable plaster. Use a paintbrush to clear away the final debris and dust.

STEP 2

Pack filler into the crack, then remove any excess and smooth the surface with a wallpaper scraper. Follow the instructions on the filler packaging.

STEP 3

Once the filler has dried, use fine sandpaper to smooth the surface and make sure the filler is flush with the wall. Ta-da! No more cracks!

PAINTING THE CEILING

Once your ceiling is clean, dry, smooth and ready, and your floor and any remaining furniture is protected, roll up your sleeves! It's finally time to get busy with the painting. How do you want to paint? Some people prefer to use a roller because it makes painting large areas really fast; others think a brush is best because you waste less paint, they are easier to clean and you don't get splatters all over your glasses/face/hands. Ultimately, it's horses for courses. Do whatever feels right for you.

Jay's Top Tip

Read the instructions and guidance on your paint tin! You might be thinking, 'Duh! Obviously, Jay!' but it's a crucial step. Drying times vary between paint types and manufacturers, as does whether you need an undercoat or primer.

If you're not sure you can achieve a smooth, neat 'line' at the edge of the ceiling, use decorator's tape at the top of the wall. The edge of the ceiling is the place to start: use a brush and paint carefully to the edge, making sure to spread the paint evenly. You might have heard of the phrase 'cutting in'? Well, that's what you need to do here. Work the paintbrush strokes at a 45-degree angle to the edge of the ceiling, so that you end up with a feathered edge to your newly painted section.

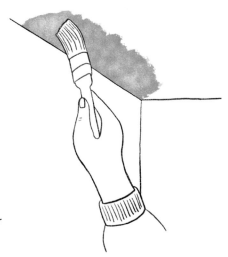

Then, once you've done the edge (and worked around any light fittings in the ceiling), use a larger brush or roller to paint the rest of the ceiling.

PAINTING THE WALLS

The method for painting walls is basically the same as for the ceiling. Start at the edges with a brush, angling your strokes into the main part of the wall, to cut into where you'll use a roller or bigger brush to paint the central area.

Important: don't be tempted to keep painting over the same bits if you think the paint is looking a bit patchy. At this not-quite-dry stage, you're more likely to be taking paint off the wall than putting more on! Bide your time, have a cuppa and wait until the wall is dry before deciding whether you need another coat or not. If you're lucky, that early patchiness will disappear as the paint dries.

PAINTING THE WOODWORK

Touch wood (pun intended!) you may find that simply washing your skirting boards and door frames will be enough. However, if they do need repainting, or you want to change the colour, always leave it until after you've tackled the ceiling and walls. It's a golden rule of decorating: start at the top and work down.

You'll need gloss, satin or eggshell paint for the woodwork, which is thicker and better able to take the knocks and bashes of day-to-day life than the emulsion you use on your walls and ceilings. The different available finishes means it doesn't have to look shiny. See page 130 for more on the different levels of shine.

You'll need to sand down the old paint to create a 'key' on the surface for the new paint to stick to. A light sanding will do, but make sure you get off any dust with a damp cloth, then let the surface dry before you start painting. Most gloss-paint manufacturers recommend applying a primer coat first – but, again, check the instructions on the tin. And follow them!

Wallpaper

There is a fantastic range of wallpapers available these days. You really can get something to suit every taste, room and budget. And you don't have to restrict it to its usual purpose – why not use wallpaper on the underside of tables, behind bookshelves, inside a display cabinet or beneath the glass on a glass-topped table?

Even if you do the traditional thing and hang the wallpaper on your walls, you don't have to cover the whole space. A single papered panel in the centre of a wall can give a whole new dimension to a room. Trust me – it can transform humble wallpaper into a work of art!

WORKING WITH PATTERN

Be careful; when you look at wallpaper samples or brochures, it's easy to get carried away with glorious patterns that look great in someone else's house. I'm all for going wild with patterned wallpaper, if that's your thing, but think about the scale of the pattern and how it'll look in your living room. A small-scale pattern in a medium-to-big room won't have much impact and can become more of a background texture. A large-scale pattern in a small room can be really IN YOUR FACE! Now, if those are the effects that you want, good on you, but think it through carefully before you get to work.

The other thing to bear in mind is the style of the pattern. A modern, geometric wallpaper might look out of whack if your furniture style is antique. Mixing different styles can look great, but keep in mind what the overall effect on the room will be.

WORKING WITH COLOUR

Most wallpaper manufacturers will recommend paint colours that go with each of their products. They're generally a safe bet. They often suggest a neutral cream or grey that is the same as one of the background colours in the paper; a stronger colour that picks out a small, coloured element of the pattern, and a contrast colour that might not be in the pattern but will resonate well with it. However, don't be limited by manufacturers' recommendations. Use your eyes and your instincts. Look around you – have you been in a café, hotel or shop with the sort of look you're after?

As always, my advice is to plan carefully. Get some samples, prop them up around the walls and see what the colours look like in your actual living room. Put the wallpaper samples next to your paint choices, furniture, cushions, carpet . . . basically, make sure that you're sure.

A big point: once you're happy with your choice, you need to order the correct number of rolls! For patterned wallpaper, you must match the pattern on each drop (strip of paper).

The bigger the distance between each 'repeat', as it is known, the more wallpaper you could end up wasting. As with paint, it's better to over-order and then return a roll or two for a refund than to run out with only two more drops left to do.

HOW TO HANG WALLPAPER

There are lots of different types of wallpaper but, essentially, they all involve a roll of paper that you need to stick to your wall in precisely placed vertical strips. Always read the instructions on the roll packaging for what type of adhesive to use. Prepare your walls in the same way as for painting (see page 91), so they are clean, dry and smooth.

Step *by* Step

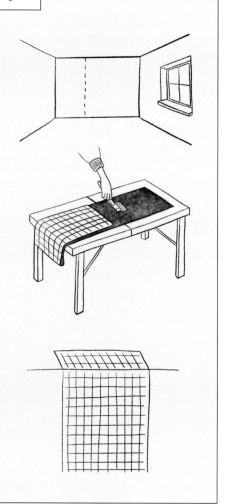

STEP 1

Start papering in the centre of the wall - or, if you have a feature such as a chimney breast, start in the middle of that. Use a plumb bob and string or a long spirit level to mark a perfectly vertical line down the wall. Careful! Easy does it!

STEP 2

Prepare your first length of wallpaper as per the instructions so it is ready to stick to the wall. Make sure you know which way is 'up', so the pattern is pointing the right way. Remember: you need to cut a slightly longer length than the wall, so the paper extends a few centimetres above and below the top and bottom, which will be trimmed later.

STEP 3

Carefully transfer the paper from the pasting table or working surface to the wall. Align it with your marked vertical line and press in place using a wallpaper hanging brush, working from the top downwards and outwards as you move towards the bottom of the strip.

I can't stress enough how important it is to use a sharp blade for trimming wallpaper at the top and bottom. It will be a little damp from the paste, and so much more prone to tearing if your knife blade is anything other than super sharp. Mind your fingers and retract the blade after use.

Step *by* Step

STEP 4

Smooth the paper out and encourage any air bubbles out to the side, then use a craft or utility knife to trim the excess paper at the ceiling and skirting board.

STEP 5

Your second drop needs to butt up to the vertical edge of the first and match the pattern perfectly. Hold up a piece, and once you're confident about this, cut the paper for the second drop and repeat the fixing process.

STEP 6

If you have obstacles to paper 'around', such as light switches, cut an opening in the paper in an 'x' shape from the centre of the obstacle to each corner, folding the resultant flaps outwards so you can paste the paper flat around the object. Trim the flaps off with a sharp craft or utility knife or scissors once it's pasted in place.

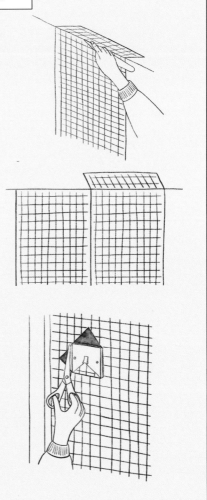

Decals, Posters & Other Wall Decoration

It's not just wallpaper that can add instant life and zest to your walls, there are loads of other options, even ignoring the paint effects that were so popular in the 1980s (rag-rollering anyone? Stencilled border?). Here's a good thing: a lot of these wall decorations are temporary. So if you're renting a gaff, they're a great way to stamp your mark on the place, then remove it easily when you move out.

DECALS

These are basically vinyl stickers that stick to your wall super-well but are also dead easy to peel off again. There are tons of options: video-game graphics, flowers, cartoon characters – you name it. They're fantastic for children's rooms: as your kids grow up, you can change the look without having to redecorate the whole room.

›› How to work with decals

It's the same advice as ever: plan, plan, plan. Then plan a bit more. If you've got a few decals to use, sketch out how they will work together in the room before you buy them. Once you've got them, cut around each element while it's still on its backing and sticky tack each bit in place on your wall to see if you like how it looks. You CAN reposition them once they're properly stuck down, but they never adhere as well once they've been peeled off and stuck down again.

WALL MURALS

Fancy an amazing whole-wall image in your home? Back in the day, the only way to get one would have been to paint it yourself. Now, though, you can get gigantic mural posters made to fit the size of your wall.

These murals come in big but manageable pieces; large sheets that you paste to the wall like wallpaper. Don't like any of the images? Well, get your own photo or artwork printed for some bespoke wall art!

If you want to do this in your living room, choose the wall with the least furniture in front of it and the fewest interruptions, such as light switches, windows or radiators. Don't forget to consider how light or dark your room is – and the effect and atmosphere that your mural will create. Bear in mind that an eight-foot pic of your mum might be a bit much!

FABRIC OPTIONS

Before wallpaper and matt emulsion paint were invented, people stuck tapestries or big rugs on their walls. As well as looking good, it was a great way to make the cold stone walls of your medieval castle feel cosy.

Now, I'm having a guess here that you don't live in a castle, but you can still use textiles to decorate your walls. Handmade quilts can give a cosy traditional feel. Vintage embroidered tablecloths can look great too. Think about the textiles you've got squirrelled away. Would they look better on the wall rather than on a table, bed or chair?

For any type of fabric wall-hanging, it's best to create a sleeve on the back, at the top, into which you can insert a wooden or metal pole. The fabric will then hang straight. You can either attach picture wire to the pole and hang the textile that way, or put hooks in your wall to hold the ends of the pole.

Jay's
Top Tip

If you want to do this in your living room, choose the wall with the least furniture in front of it and the fewest interruptions, such as light switches, windows or radiators.

Lighting Styles

For me, it's dead important to have different lighting options in your living room. You do so many things in there! It needs to be bright and light when you want to hang out with friends and family, and nice and subdued when you fancy a chill-out zone to listen to music or watch TV. Plus, what about when you are playing with the kids? Trust me, subtle mood lighting is not a good idea when you're building Lego or having a game of Uno!

MAIN LIGHT

Most homes will have a light in the centre of the ceiling in every room, or spotlights set into the ceiling, and possibly some wall lights as well. It's up to you how bright or dark you want to make them. Changing your bulbs can alter not only the brightness but the warmth or coolness of the light in the room.

>> Wattage and lumens

If you were born in the last century – i.e. you're an old girl or geezer, like me – then you grew up thinking about light bulb 'strength' in terms of watts. Time to get with the plot! Now the old filament bulbs are history, it's better to rate them by the light they give out (lumens, or Lm) and not the energy they consume (watts, or w). An old-fashioned 40w bulb gives off light equal to 360Lm; 60w is 600Lm and 100w is 1100Lm.

TASK LIGHTING

This is lighting that you need when doing certain tasks like reading, doing a crossword or knitting. You usually get this from a lamp – either a table lamp, if you have a side table or sideboard in your living room, or a freestanding standard lamp, or both. Typically, these are best positioned at the sides of a room with the main light in the centre.

That's not the only way to do it, though! A central light fitting can work as task lighting. You just need the sort that have several long wires hanging from a central point. Each bulb can be moved to dangle over specific areas, secured by a hook. I think of these fittings as being like an octopus with a light bulb at the end of each tentacle! But maybe that's just me . . .

MOOD LIGHTING

Now, this is my favourite sort of lighting! It gives out the least light and lets you sit back and chill. You can create mood lighting by putting one task light on and sitting on the other side of the room. Simple, but effective! Or, if you've got a lamp with a moveable shade, you might be able to angle it away from you to diffuse the direct light.

For me, though, the very best sort of mood lighting comes from candles. There's something about the mellow yellow light and flickering flames that I find so calming. It takes me to my happy place. You can use a few big candles or a cluster of tealights. Either way, I'd really recommend it.

Obviously, candles are not the best idea if you've got toddlers or pets wandering around. Plus, after a couple of drinks, you've got to be careful not to leave lit candles unattended! But you're not daft. You know that already . . .

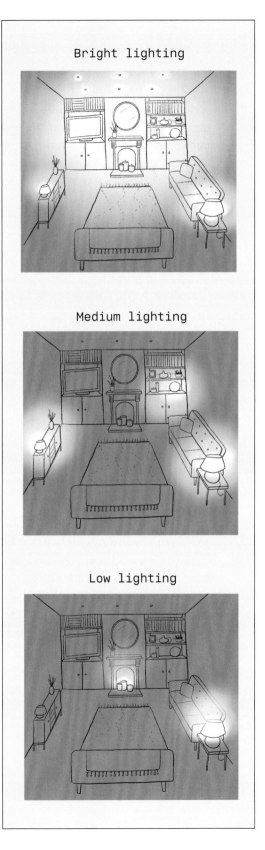

Bright lighting

Medium lighting

Low lighting

Comfortable Seating

A living room isn't a living room unless you can sit in it comfortably and relax. What you park your bum on is up to you. Obviously, most people have sofas and armchairs, but floor cushions or beanbags are also good options, especially for the younger members of the family. There's a good reason why living rooms are also called sitting rooms – it's what we do the most when we're in them!

SOFAS

Sofas come in every kind of shape and size and I guarantee you will find something that will suit your room, your needs and your budget. It might take a bit of hunting down, mind you, so be prepared for that!

Well, rather than spending weeks or even months sitting on every sofa in every furniture shop within a fifty-mile radius, I recommend having a good initial think about the size, shape and colour that you're after. Traditional two- or three-seater? L-shaped? Modular? Possibly has a double use as a bed for overnight guests? Storage? Reclining function? These decisions will all help you to narrow down the options.

Think about the length of a sofa. I'm quite a tall bloke and I like to put my feet up and lie on the sofa if I'm in the mood. Basically, a two-seater is never going to cut the mustard for me. Yet some people find long, three- or four-seater sofas decidedly un-cosy. Bigger isn't always better for everyone.

>> Social sofas

If you want to sit and socialize in your living room a lot, you don't want all of your friends and family to be strung out side by side on one sofa like a bus queue! It's not conducive to being able to look at each other while you're chatting away. Corner or curved sofas are way better for positioning people in a more easily sociable way.

If you have visitors dropping by regularly, it is handy to have some ad hoc seating available to add to your usual sofa and armchairs in the living room. Beanbags and floor cushions are great for this, and so are pouffes and footstools.

Sample sofa configurations

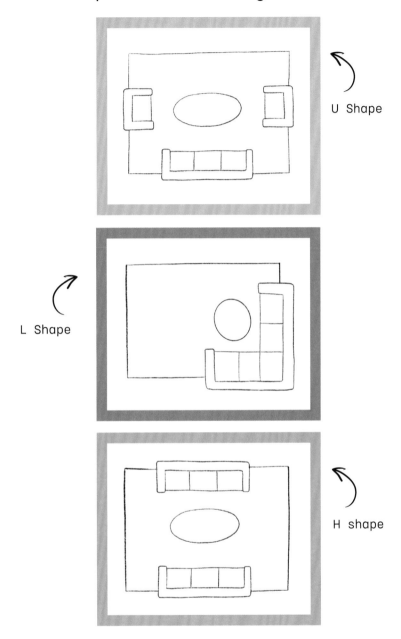

U Shape

L Shape

H shape

ARMCHAIRS

If you've got a fairly big living room, armchairs are a great way to make the space feel cosy. They do tend to take up more space per seat than a sofa, but they create a sociable seating arrangement when they're placed opposite or at an angle to a sofa.

You can treat yourself and really go to town in choosing your dream chair. Just don't blow a gasket when you keep finding your partner, kids or dog have nabbed it before you!

UPHOLSTERY

So. Many. Choices! Before we get onto colour and pattern, we need to start with fabric. There are pros and cons to each one, so here's a simple summary:

	PROS	CONS
LEATHER/ FAUX LEATHER	Wipe-clean, hardwearing, classic choice that will stand the test of time	Can be cold to sit on at first, can stick to the skin if you're in shorts
SUEDE/ FAUX SUEDE	Feels good, looks good, hardwearing if treated carefully	Can stain or mark easily
VELVET	Soft to the touch, luxury feel, opulent colours	Gathers pet hair easily; can be hard to clean
COTTON	Usually washable, smooth texture doesn't pick up pet hair	Budget versions with low thread count can wear out quickly
POLYESTER	Huge range of colours, patterns, textures and finishes; often washable	Can look a bit synthetic and unnatural
WOOL/WOOL BLEND	Looks great, feels cosy	Can stain and needs professional cleaning

COLOUR AND PATTERN

Obviously, you're going to want to choose a colour and perhaps a pattern that you love, and that look good with the rest of your décor. But, early doors, have a think about colour tone and pattern scale from a practical point of view. What gets spilled most often in your home? Do you have a dog that jumps on the sofa with muddy paws? Are there toddlers about who smear yoghurt handprints everywhere? Be honest about these basic questions and it will save you future grief.

Once you've got a few ideas about what your sofa might get splodged with, it might be wise to aim your colour choices towards a similar tone. Beige is terrible for red wine but not bad for muddy paws. Palest blue is awful for muddy paws but not a disaster for yoghurty fingers. Rich purple is horrendous for yoghurty fingers but pretty good for red wine.

In the same way, when it comes to pattern, a small-scale design can work well to hide any splodges and won't make a big visual impact unless the colours you go for are LOUD. Large-scale patterns can be really WOW!, which is great if that's what you're after, but could get in the way of a more chilled-out vibe.

If you've chosen a patterned upholstery fabric, take a moment to think about how the design will work with the shape and style of the furniture. Modern geometrics might clash with a curvy shape. Mid-century modern furniture style might not work too well with a country toile pattern. Always keep the big picture in mind.

Jay's
Top Tip

If you're buying a new sofa that has removable covers, it's worth finding out how much a second set of covers in a different colour or pattern would cost. It can extend the life of your sofa by years if you share the wear-and-tear (and spills!) between two sets of covers.

Reupholstery Basics

Reupholstering an entire fixed-cover chair or sofa is a big job and definitely one that's best left to the professionals. I am one and, believe you me, it's not a job that you take on lightly!

If your sofa is sagging in the middle or looks lopsided, it's likely that work needs to be done on the springs or frame, which will require specialist tools and knowledge. However, if it's a case of fabric needing to be replaced, you can successfully do it yourself. All you need is time, patience and a sewing machine.

LOOSE COVERS

A lot of modern sofas have removable covers. You can take them off and wash them in the washing machine or take them to the dry cleaners. But what you can also do in this situation is use them as a template for new fabric.

Depending on your covers, it's possible you could do this without taking them apart. Remember to leave a good seam allowance on upholstery fabric, and trace around each shape carefully. Look at the way each cover is constructed and you should be able to work out which parts were sewn together first.

If you don't want to keep the existing covers, by far the best way to get a good result is to unpick them carefully and use the individual pieces as templates. If you're in luck, you can even reuse the zips, if they're in decent nick.

FIXED COVERS

If the fabric on your furniture isn't removable, you can still make your own loose covers to fit over your existing seat pads and sofa frame, but it takes some careful planning.

Once you take into account the time it will take you, plus the cost of materials, you could find that it's better to hire a professional to do this work for you. However, if you do want to DIY, here is a basic guide to thinking about your chair or sofa in terms of separate fabric pieces, and measuring for them.

It's important to figure out where to put zips or other fastenings, too. If your sofa backs onto a wall then fastenings should go at the back, where they won't be seen. However, if the sofa is visible from all sides, working invisible zips into side seams is likely to look better.

Putting seams along sharp angles will accentuate them

Placing the zips along the back corner edges will give a really neat finish

Treat each separate facet as a separate shape

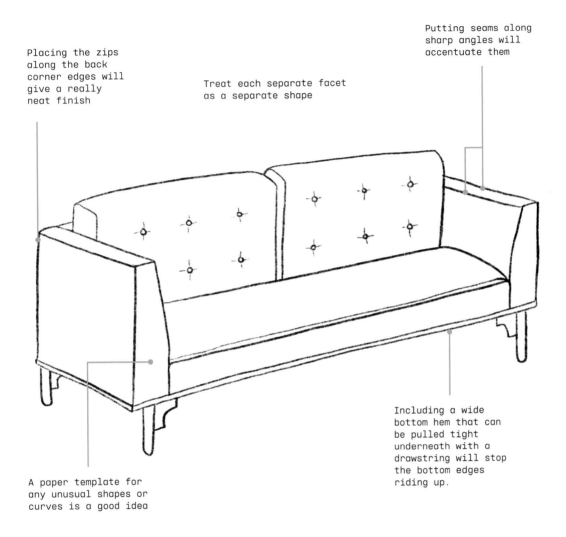

A paper template for any unusual shapes or curves is a good idea

Including a wide bottom hem that can be pulled tight underneath with a drawstring will stop the bottom edges riding up.

Jay's Top Tip

Furniture nowadays always has flame-retardant fabric, so make sure that when you're replacing covers the fabric you choose meets these safety standards. If it doesn't, you'll need to have it treated with a fire-retardant coating.

Cushions & Blankets

I love all the soft, cuddly living-room accessories! They make you feel comfortable and cossetted, as well as adding colours and textures to your room. But it's about scale as well as quantity – you can have too much of a good thing!

CUSHION PADS

The insides of cushions are usually filled with either feathers or synthetic fibres, although you can also get wool-filled ones. Feather ones are heavier and some people are allergic to them; hollow- or microfibre and wool pads are usually springier. It all comes down to budget and personal preference. You can buy these plain pads from plenty of places. Just make sure you figure out the best sizes and shapes for your furniture first.

CUSHION COVERS

Here's where you can get really creative without having to make a long-term commitment! Adding an accent colour or a wild pattern in scatter-cushion form is a cheap and easy way to try something new and refresh your living-room look.

Fancy trying something attention-grabbing? Go for it! Go wild with faux fur, add festive sparkle with sequins, or make personalized cushions for your friends and family. Remember to always buy washable covers if you've got pets, kids or – worst of all – messy adults in the house.

≫ Simple envelope cushion covers

This method for making your own cushion covers has no fastenings, such as buttons or zips, so it's quick, easy and budget-friendly! You need to allow a bit of extra fabric to create the overlapping envelope opening at the back. It's best to use proper home-décor-weight fabric here, which is thicker and tougher than dressmaking fabric and will hold its shape well and stand up better to wear and tear.

STEP 1

Choose a cushion pad and note its dimensions. Your fabric needs to be a little wider to allow for a 1.5cm seam allowance on each side.

STEP 2

Measure and cut your fabric, ideally as a single piece. Take note: for a 40cm cushion you'll need the fabric to be 43cm wide (40 + 1.5 + 1.5) and at least 110cm long (40 front + 40 back + 20 for overlap and 10 for hems).

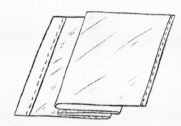

STEP 3

If your fabric is prone to fraying, it's a good idea to sew a zigzag-stitch all around the raw edges of the rectangle. Then pin and stitch a 2.5cm hem at one end of the rectangle, and a 7.5cm hem at the other end.

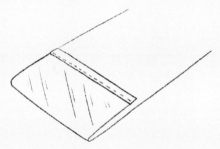

STEP 4

Time to get folding! With the right side of the fabric facing uppermost, measure 30cm in from the end with the larger hem, and fold it over at that point towards the middle. Pin down the sides to secure.

STEP 5

Measure 40cm from the first fold, then fold the end with the smaller hem over at that point and pin in place. There should be about 10cm of overlap in the centre back of the cushion.

STEP 6

Stitch down the sides, leaving a 1.5cm seam allowance. Turn the cushion cover the right way out, and squeeze your cushion pad inside. Plump it up, sit on it and feel pleased with yourself!

BLANKETS

Much as I hate clutter, it's handy to have a blanket or two available in the living room for chilly evenings, or for when you just need that little bit of extra comfort. Knitted, woven, quilted . . . there's a favourite blanket out there for everyone, or you can always take the plunge and make your own.

Traditional blankets are woven woollen cloth, often with stitching around the edges to stop the fabric fraying. Here's a quick history lesson for you: although people have used such coverings to keep warm for thousands of years, the word 'blanket' comes from the name of a Bristol weaver who made soft woollen cloth in the fourteenth century. Cheers, Thomas Blanquette!

Now, you're not Thomas Blanquette and you're probably not going to weave your own woollen fabric, but you could add your own stitching around the edge of a modern blanket or piece of cosy fabric to suit your living-room colour scheme. Choose yarn that's thick enough to create the effect you want, but not so thick that it's hard for a big enough needle to pass through the fabric.

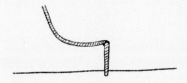

STEP 1

Thread your needle with an arm's length of yarn. Make sure you have plenty: you'll probably need several lengths to get all the way around your blanket. Knot the end of the yarn and overstitch at the edge of the blanket to make a neat starting point.

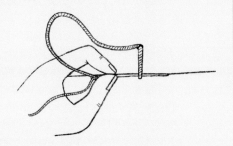

STEP 2

Push the needle under the yarn at the edge of the blanket to anchor it in position ready for the first proper blanket stitch.

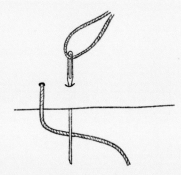

STEP 3

Poke the needle through the cloth at the point where you want the bottom of the next 'leg' to be. As you pull the needle through, make sure the loop of yarn is behind it.

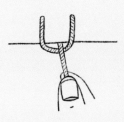

STEP 4

Pull all the loose yarn through to form the stitch – don't pull so tight that the fabric edge buckles, but do pull tight enough that the stitch takes shape.

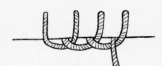

STEP 5

Carry on like this, either keeping the stitches regular or varying the lengths of the 'legs' for a different, more rustic look. To join a new length of yarn, just knot the new piece tightly to the end of the old piece, with the knot positioned very close to the cloth, where the yarn comes through from back to front.

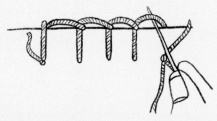

STEP 6

Put the needle through the top of the previous loop and pull the new thread through, completing the previous stitch with the new yarn. And keep going till you're finished!

Fireplaces

A living-room fireplace gives you a great opportunity to be creative. Perhaps you've even got a working fire or log burner, too – lovely for winter evenings. Just make sure your chimney is professionally cleaned regularly and be careful what you burn. Some areas have regulations about the sort of fuel that can and can't be used, so check with your council before buying. Take a look at some of the non-traditional eco alternatives, too. You can get 'logs' made from coffee grinds that burn well and don't give off as many harmful gases as actual wood. I bet you didn't know that, eh? !

MAKING A FIRE

Cavemen could do it dead easy, but can we? Making a fire is pretty primal and the sort of thing that we probably all think everybody knows how to do but, in reality, not many people really do!

Well, don't worry. Like everything in this world, it's easy when you know how. The main thing you need to remember is that you have to layer your combustible materials from easy-to-light fast burn at the base to takes-a-while-to-get-going slow burn above. Remember that golden rule and you'll soon have flames.

STEP 1

Clean out the grate and make sure the ashes tray underneath isn't full. You need the air to be able to circulate so that the fire can burn. Scrumple up old newspaper and put a layer of it on the grate.

STEP 2

Lay kindling or thin, dry sticks in a spaced-out grid on top of the paper. Think about air circulation – you need lots of gaps!

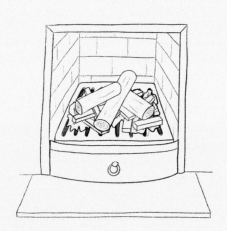

STEP 3

Top layer: use logs either on top of the kindling or resting against it, angled like a tepee (again, it's all about air circulation). As the paper and kindling burn, the logs will lower down towards the grate like a, well, collapsing tepee!

STEP 4

Light the paper at the bottom in several places. Keep an eye on the fire and, once the logs are alight and the other material has burned down, add more logs as needed.

MANTELPIECE

Call me Sherlock Blades, but if you've got a fireplace the chances are you've also got a mantelpiece. This strong, slimline shelf can be a great place for displaying precious items and is the perfect height for candles or tealights, or the ideal location for a big mirror to reflect the daylight around the room. But what if the mantelpiece you've got doesn't suit your aesthetic?

Well, painting it is probably the easiest option or, if it's a real eyesore to you and your family, you could take it out. However, before you do any of that, check how old your mantelpiece and fire surround is, and think about whether it is a 'period feature' in your home. If it's antique but you still definitely don't want to keep it, you can probably flog it. Go down to your local architectural salvage yard armed with a photo of it and have a chat with them.

HOLE IN THE WALL

Over the years, I've seen all kinds of creative things done with the 'hole in the wall' where a fire would once have burned before the days of central heating. There is so much fun you can have with them!

I saw a really cool fish tank installation in a hole in the wall once. It looked brilliant. Another time, someone I knew fitted out their old fireplace as their dog's bed. The dog loved it, even if it was a bit weird for visitors to see the mutt climbing happily into a fireplace.

My favourite use of an old fireplace space is to put a beautiful object in it and shine a spotlight on it. It can look like having a sculpture on display in a museum! The fireplace acts as a frame for whatever you want to display, and it can look really cool and arresting.

At the end of the day, it's up to you to make the most of your hole in the wall. Logs stacked up can look great. Flickering candles are a great option. You can even use the area for something seasonal that gets changed as you move through the year. If you're lucky enough to have it, it's a great space – don't waste it!

MAKING MORE SPACE

One last thought on fireplaces. If you've got a chimney breast in your living room that you're not using, and you're short on space, you can have the whole breast removed.

This is definitely a job for a professional, though – if the chimney breast is intact and the chimney itself is still in place, then either the whole lot needs to come out or steel supports need to be installed to take the weight of the chimney breast upstairs and the chimney stack above that. It's a big job, but it can be worth it to get a bit more space and a flat wall.

My Favourite...

HI-FI AND CD SHELVING

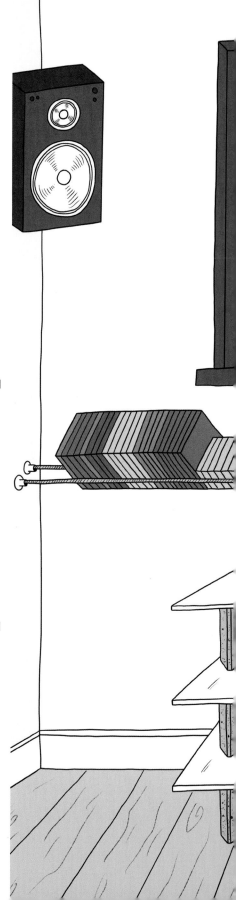

Music and design are the two biggest things in my life. I love them both. I can't think of a time when I'm happier than when I'm listening to some banging roots – reggae or soul – while kicking back in a bit of my home that I've got exactly how I want it.

That made it all the sweeter when I had a blinding idea (if I can say so myself!) for how to combine the two and show off my hi-fi and my CD collection in a way that looked totally fantastic. And all I needed was some wire, concrete blocks from the garden and some old glass shelves! I picked the gear up here and there. The breeze blocks were shaped like hexagons and were lying around my garden. The glass shelves had been inside display cabinets in an old gentlemen's outfitters. They were proper, hefty toughened glass: four feet long and half-an-inch thick.

I stacked the breeze blocks in my living room and put pieces of glass in between. My hi-fi went on there in layers (hey, it was the olden days!), then I used two tensioned wires fixed across the room above the hi-fi to put my cassette tapes and CDs on. The way I positioned the wires meant the CDs sat at 45 degrees and looked like they were floating. It all looked amazing! The wall behind was painted white, so when you walked in the room you couldn't really see the shelves or the wires, and it looked like the music centre and CDs were suspended in mid-air! It blew all my mates away: 'Bloody hell, Jay? How did you do that?'

It made lying on the sofa and listening to Bob Marley or Gregory Isaacs all the sweeter. Then I got vexed that the CD spines were all different colours, which looked too messy, so I moved the CDs and just kept the tapes there because they were all the same brand of recordable ones, with white inserts. What, a bit over the top? Me? I have no idea what you're talking about . . .

Hallway

& Stairs

First impressions are important, whether it's meeting someone or going into a house you've not visited before.

You can spend ages doing up your front room or your kitchen, which is great, but it's easy to forget that your hallway is the gateway that welcomes people to your home.

Well, actually, there's something even before that – your front door! I want to talk about doors a little in this chapter (although there's more in the Outdoor Spaces chapter too) because they send out the very first signal about your home. If your door's a mess, with peeling paint and a knob hanging off, visitors might think, nah, I'm not going in there!

But assuming your door is cushty, your hallway is the first clue people get as to what the rest of your house is like. It's such an important space. In fact, I'd go as far as to say that the hallway and stairs are the most badly neglected – and underestimated – areas in most homes.

I can understand why. Kitchens and bathrooms and bedrooms are all destination rooms that have a purpose. Hallways and stairs are merely a means of getting there. They're places that you pass through on the way from A to B, so it's easy to assume that they're nothing special.

Well, I don't agree. I think hallways and stairs are everything, and they're very special.

Think about it. So much happens in a hallway! It's where you go first when you get home and might be greeted with a kiss. It's where you pack your kids off to school from in the morning, or confront them when they've been out and got home too late. It's a major space, so why should you neglect it?

When I was a kid, the hallway was almost the heart of the house. It was where I'd spend hours sitting on the stairs, talking to my mates on the landline phone (remember them?). My mum would spend even longer nattering with my grandma or my aunty, then hand me the phone to say hello to them: 'Oh, Mum! Have I got to?'

The hallway doesn't serve that purpose any more but it's still the heart of the home in other ways. It's the centre of comings and goings, the place where you bump into each other on the way in and out, and have a word or a quick hug. So you want it to be warm and welcoming.

My first stipulation for a hallway is that it has to be clean and tidy. You have probably

I think the important thing is to minimize clutter while still having everything you need to hand.

gathered by this point in the book that I hate clutter, and this is as true here as anywhere else. In fact, it's probably truer here than anywhere else.

If you're getting home from a mad day in a busy job, possibly after a lousy commute, the last thing you need is to walk into a busy, messy hallway. You want to get home, chill and relax, not get more agitated and stressed having to step over stuff that is lying around. It's my personal taste, but when I see hallways full of benches and shoe racks, with loads of coats hanging up on the wall, I think they are way too busy. Your home should feel like a sanctuary, not like walking into a clothes store's overcrowded stock room!

I think the important thing is to minimize clutter while still having everything you need to hand. Can you put a cupboard under your stairs to keep coats in, out of view? I turned my understairs area in one house into drawers! I'll talk more about that on page 148.

It's tempting to get home and dump your bag and keys by the door, but if everyone in the house does that, it soon starts to look like a junk shop! So, why not use your DIY skills to create a couple of cool storage boxes? They're easy to make and, believe you me, they make such difference.

Like anywhere in the house, imagination is everything. In one place I lived in, rather than a traditional stairway banister, we used a felled tree branch and hooked it along the wall next to the stairs. I'll tell you how on page 127; it was simple to do and it looked absolutely amazing.

So, how do you approach home décor in this crucial part of the house? Is it a place for pictures, or mirrors? Do you want bright colours on your walls, or something softer and more understated? And how do you handle what can become the bane of your DIY life – spindles?

There's a lot you can do to make sure that you, your family and your visitors walk into your home and immediately feel at ease and pleased to be there. Here are my hints for a happy hallway.

Hall & Stairs Woodwork

The hallway and stairs take quite a buffeting in any home. There's a lot of wear and tear. The family are always passing through on the way from one room to another, and anything big that gets brought into the house comes in this way, too. Those poor skirting boards can take a beating and your stair banisters tend to need fairly regular TLC if they're going to stay looking pukka.

SKIRTING BOARDS

It's thought that it was the Victorians who first came up with the idea of skirting boards. Back in those days, they offered a great solution to three common issues.

The first was the messy join between the bottom of the wall and the floor. Old-style plaster was much rougher than what we're used to nowadays, and getting a neat finish where wall met floor was a rare thing.

Secondly, houses in those days didn't have damp proof courses. This meant rising damp would often make the bottom of walls look pretty iffy and, worse still, smell pretty whiffy!

Thirdly, the wear and tear resulting from people's feet, bags and furniture constantly bashing against the bottom of walls led to a knocked-about finish that was definitely more shabby than chic.

So, some clever Victorian came up with the idea of attaching wooden boards along the bottom of each wall to hide the messy plasterwork and the rising damp, plus offer protection against wear and tear. Bosh! Sorted!

Of all these issues, the only ones relevant to skirting boards these days is protecting the bottom of the walls from damage. The wood boards are more hardwearing than the plaster finish of any wall, but they can get dented and their paintwork or varnish usually gets chipped over time. More commonly, though, they just need a really good clean to spruce them up. Like all of us!

» Cleaning painted wood

OK, this really isn't rocket science, but you might need to think laterally when it comes to getting into the nooks and crannies of your skirtings, spindles, windowsills and any other painted woodwork in the home. Here are my top tips:

Jay's Top Tips

1 Get all of the dust and grime off using your vacuum attachment (the brush one usually works well).

2 Use some warm soapy water and a soft cloth to wipe every part of the woodwork. Don't use anything abrasive, as you don't want to damage the gloss paint surface, but make sure you put some elbow grease in!

3 For difficult nooks and crannies, try using cotton buds or an old toothbrush dipped in warm soapy water to really get in there.

4 If you're left with any marks or scuffs that won't budge with soapy water, try using something acidic such as vinegar or lemon juice, or even a magic eraser sponge.

BANISTERS

Almost all staircases will have a banister rail. It's a helpful safety feature to give you something to hold on to as you go up and down the stairs. It's just a practical aid, right? Right – but practical doesn't have to mean boring.

A banister can be made from anything that is long and straight enough to attach to your wall (or to the top of your spindles, if you have them). You can buy handrails made from all kinds of wood, then oil, varnish or paint them, or you can use a length of thick rope or metal. If you want to be really fancy, you can even get handrails with LED lights embedded in them so you can see the stair treads at night without having to put the overhead light on.

As I mentioned earlier, the best banister I ever installed was made from a felled tree branch that I got for free. It happened to be fairly straight, and as soon as I saw it, I knew it would make the perfect handrail for our stairs. I let it dry out properly at home then stripped off the bark to reveal the most beautiful, smooth wood. A bit of Danish oil gave it a lovely natural finish.

» Installing a non-standard handrail

The most important thing to remember if you're going off-piste with a banister is . . . SAFETY FIRST! As long as your chosen rail is strong, and it's possible to fix it to the wall in a way that makes it sturdy, you'll be on the right track.

Jay's Top Tip

In the UK, it's the law that you have to have a banister on any staircase after the first two steps, and it must be positioned between 90cm and 1m above the stair treads. If your staircase is wider than 1m, you need a handrail on each side.

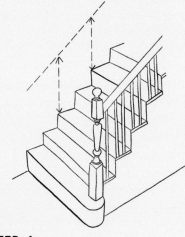

STEP 1

Choose the right brackets to suit your handrail and your wall, and lightly mark a straight line along the wall, between 90cm and 1m up from the step below. Use a piece of masking tape for this.

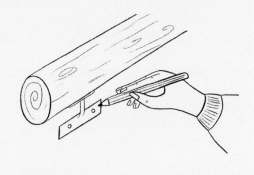

STEP 2

Get the family involved! Round up some helpers and ask them to hold the handrail in position. Place each of the brackets in turn on the wall along your line, then mark both handrail and wall with where you need to drill holes.

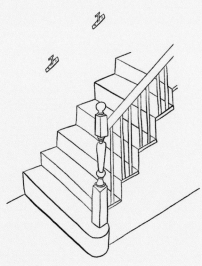

STEP 3

Attach the brackets to the wall, ensuring you use the right wall plugs and screws for your particular wall (see pages 30–31).

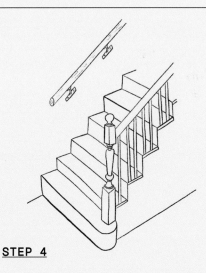

STEP 4

Place the handrail back on the brackets and check that the marks for where to drill align. If you need to adjust your marks, do so. Drill starter holes in the handrail (remember to change the drill bit if necessary). Screw the handrail in place – and voilà! Job done!

REMOVING GLOSS PAINT

Sometimes there are so many layers of old paint on skirting boards, banisters and spindles (or any woodwork, for that matter) that the best course of action is to strip it off. Once you've done that, you can either get a natural wood finish, by oiling or varnishing what's under all that paint, or paint it afresh.

Before you start, though, it's crucial to test whether the old paint contains any lead, as this will need careful and specialist removal. It's important to remember that the lead-containing paint could be several layers under. You can buy testing kits for lead in paint at DIY stores or online (see page 46 for more detail on paint-stripping options and methods), but be warned – it can be a time-consuming job, especially on spindles.

PAINTING BARE WOODWORK

If you've got new, untreated wood, you'll need to seal any knots first. The knots in the wood are where the branches would have been, so this is where the grain of the wood changes – they are usually round or oval and appear darker than the surrounding wood.

The knots also contain sap; this is what you're sealing in, so that it doesn't seep out over time and ruin your hard work. So, do these things in this order – and don't forget to read the labels on the products you use and follow the manufacturer's instructions. Here are my top tips:

1 Apply knotting solution to all knots. Usually two or three coats are needed, with around half an hour's drying time in between.

2 If there are any holes, dents or other imperfections in the wood, use wood filler to sort them out, then sand the filler smooth once it has dried.

3 Apply primer. This is crucial as it creates a perfect surface for the subsequent layers of paint to cling to. Only skip this step if your undercoat has a primer combined within it.

4 Once the primer is fully dry, apply a thin layer of undercoat, keeping it smooth and avoiding drips. You will probably need to apply a second coat of undercoat once the first is fully dry. Again, refer to your paint tin and follow the instructions.

5 Once your undercoat is fully dry it's time for the topcoat. Because of all the bang-on preparation work you've already done, you'll only need one coat. Be careful: brush in the same direction as the grain of the wood and don't apply it too thickly.

PAINTING OVER EXISTING PAINT

If a good clean hasn't spruced up your painted woodwork enough, or you want to change the colour, a fresh coat of paint is the way to go. As with so many things in life, though, it's all about the prep!

1. Use sandpaper to lightly sand all of the existing paintwork just enough to rough up the surface (see page 93).

2. Fill any cracks or holes with wood filler. Then when this has dried, sand it to give a perfectly even finish with the surrounding wood.

3. Use a damp cloth to remove all the dust created when you sanded the surface.

4. Done all that? Good! Now you're ready to rock and roll! Once the surfaces are fully dry, it's time to get painting. I know I keep saying this, but read the instructions on your paint tin. Oh, and don't forget to protect your floor from drips.

TYPES OF PAINT FOR WOODWORK

I usually refer to any paint you'd use on woodwork as gloss paint. Well, let me qualify that. There are actually several different types of paint that give different finishes. I always use water-based paints as they are better for the environment, plus they dry so much quicker. I find that oil-based gloss takes days to dry and the smell can linger for weeks. Who needs that pen-and-ink hanging around? No, thanks!

THREE MAIN TYPES OF PAINT

- **GLOSS:** This is the classic high-shine paint for woodwork, available nowadays as a water-based paint and offering a wipeable, tough finish. It does the job.

- **EGGSHELL:** As the name suggests, this paint is only a little bit shiny, like the shell of an egg. If you're painting your woodwork and walls the same colour, using eggshell for the wood can help it blend almost seamlessly with the walls while giving a wipeable, hard-wearing finish.

- **SATIN:** This has a sheen that's somewhere in between eggshell and gloss. The finish does vary a bit between manufacturers.

Hanging Pictures & Mirrors

Having a mirror in your hallway makes a lot of sense – and not just because you can check that you don't still have your breakfast egg on your chin before leaving the house for work! Hallways tend to be small spaces, and mirrors reflect what light there is to make them a bit brighter.

Do you like a lot of pictures in your home? I prefer to have just one cool picture at the top of the stairs to draw the eye and to keep the rest of the walls clean and simple, but I know a lot of people love pictures all around their hallway and up the stairs. Fair dos – this can also look great if you do it right. Like everything else, there are no right or wrong answers. It's your home – your call!

PLACEMENT OF MIRRORS

Where you put your mirror sounds simple, and it is, but a lot of people don't think about it enough. If there is more than one person in your home who will be checking for fried egg on their mush in the hallway mirror, you need to make sure it's placed at a height where everyone will be able to see themselves in it. Who wants to be leaving the house on tiptoes or bent double?

Another obvious, but crucial, point is to be careful not to position a mirror in a place that might give you, or more likely your children, a fright as you all move around the house. Think twice about putting mirrors opposite doorways: catching sight of a sudden movement can freak out young kids.

Thirdly, think closely about exactly what the mirrors will be reflecting. Position them so that they reflect aspects of your home, or the view from your windows, that you really like. It does wonders for your sense of well-being!

CHOOSING & DISPLAYING ONE FOCAL POINT IMAGE

The best thing to do is to choose one picture that you absolutely love and position it so that it draws your eye towards it. Ideally, hang it so that it can be seen from multiple places or angles: the top of the stairs is usually a great place, or anywhere in your home that has a corridor. Putting a great picture on the wall at the end of a corridor can make a boring walk much more interesting and enjoyable.

Jay's Top Tip

Putting a great picture on the wall at the end of a corridor can make a boring walk much more interesting and enjoyable.

GROUPING PICTURES IN DIFFERENT FRAME SIZES

A good trick for making this sort of display work well is to think about the spacing between the picture frames, rather than worrying about lining up the frames themselves, which might all be different sizes.

If you stick to the same-sized gap between the sides of the pictures, and opt for tops and bottoms of frames to be either aligned or very obviously not aligned, then you're likely to be well chuffed with the results. Don't go for almost-but-not-quite-lined up though, because that is never easy on the eye.

HANGING PICTURES OF THE SAME SIZE

I think this is the most difficult type of picture hanging, because you've got to be spot-on. For best results, you should turn to two old friends who never go out of fashion: a trusty pencil and paper.

Draw the planned arrangement first, with the measurements of the frames and your chosen amount of space between each. Once you've got that, you'll need to mark the top centre point of each frame, then calculate the distance between these points, both vertically and horizontally. Once you have those measurements (and don't forget to double-check 'em!), mark the wall and fix your picture hooks or nails at the correct points.

Jay's Top Tip

Draw the planned arrangement first, with the measurements of the frames and your chosen amount of space between each.

PICTURE HOOKS AND THEIR COUSINS

There are plenty of ways to fix pictures and mirrors to your walls that are suitable for different materials, frames and mirrors.

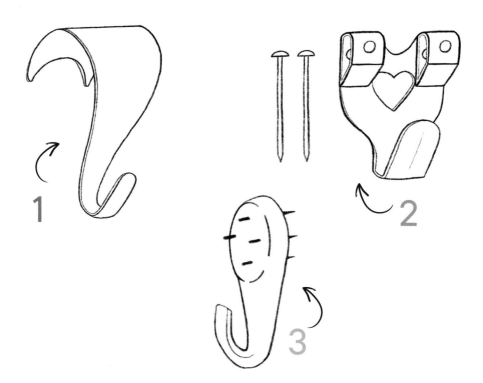

1 PICTURE HOOK RAILS

Some homes, especially period properties, have picture rails close to the top of their walls. The large metal picture-rail hooks fit snugly around the moulding and have a smaller hook at the bottom for hanging the picture from. You'll need to attach picture wire to the back of your frames at the desired length to hang them on the hook at the height you want.

2 PICTURE HOOKS (TRADITIONAL METAL)

These metal hooks have holes for their fixing nails that ensure the nails are angled slightly. It gives a much more secure wall hook than if they were hammered in straight.

3 PICTURE HOOKS (MODERN PLASTIC)

These hooks have four pins to attach them to the wall that you just hammer in, and they are surprisingly strong for their size. They work well with modern frames that have an integral hanging hook on the back.

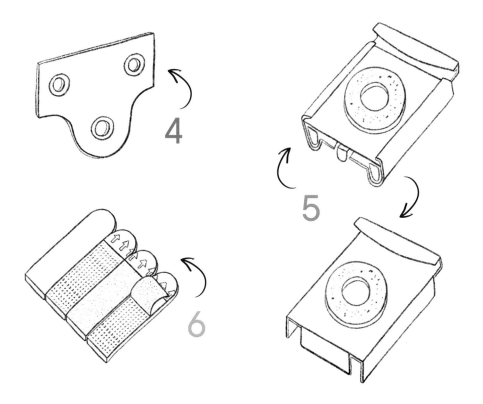

4 MIRROR PLATES

These metal plates are intended for mirrors with a wooden backing or frame. You screw one side of the plate to the back of the mirror, leaving part of the plate with one of the screw holes sticking out. You then use this screw hole to fix the mirror to the wall. Usually, a mirror will need two or even four of these fittings to make it really secure.

5 CONCEALED MIRROR FIXINGS

These fixings are for mirrors that have no frame or backing. They usually come in pairs, with the bottom fixing being solid and the top one having a spring action so you are able to insert the mirror.

6 SELF-ADHESIVE STRIPS

If you're in two minds where to have your pictures, these little guys are a brilliant solution. They're removable and don't leave any marks on your walls, but be sure to follow the manufacturer's instructions to the letter: some wall surfaces aren't suitable, and environments like steamy bathrooms can make them lose their 'stick'.

Hallway Storage

As we know, hallways are usually small spaces, which means you haven't got a lot of options when it comes to their layout. And because hallways and stairs are spaces you pass through rather than hang out and relax in, they can become a dumping ground for all sorts of stuff.

Well, don't do that! There are plenty of things you can do to maximize the space, minimize the mess and still have everything you need to hand . . .

PLAN PRACTICALLY

The key to an organized hallway is making sure that whatever needs to live there has a dedicated space. Ideally, this is out of sight in a storage box or slimline cupboard. Here's how you go about sorting that. Make a list of what you and your household really have to keep in the hall. Wherever possible, find alternative places to keep items you don't always need, such as winter coats in the summer (although, given our British summers, there are no guarantees!).

>> Mail

We all get plagued by junk mail. Don't let it pile up in your hallway, or your gaff will look like student digs! When you pick it up off your mat, take it straight to a handy place to open it, which will very likely be in your kitchen, bang next to the recycling bin. Or, even better, just put unwanted post straight into the recycling bin.

>> Keys

There are lots of good key-storage solutions. Hooks on the wall, little slimline cupboards, or just a simple bowl on a shelf all work well. A couple of words to the wise, though. Be careful about leaving keys on view from your front door, and make sure they're far enough away from your letterbox that no one is able to steal them with a magnet or hook on a pole. Yep, spot the guy who grew up in the ghetto!

>> Shoes

At the end of this chapter (see page 148), I describe my favourite storage space for shoes and other necessities. In fact, it is one of the innovative home DIY jobs that I am proudest of in my life. I still get a warm glow thinking about it. Seriously! Before we get there, though, there are plenty of other neat ways to stash your footwear. Most importantly, you need to get shoes off the floor. A shoe rack, a box, or small storage drawers are all easy-peasy to get hold of. A slimline wooden box with a lid can even double up as a bench to perch your bum on while you put your shoes on.

>> Coats

The simple rule of thumb is to keep the number of coats hanging in your hallway to the bare minimum, rather than sticking every one of the entire household's there. A tall, shallow cupboard is the best way to keep the hallway looking clutter-free. Better still, if you have an understairs cupboard, try keeping coats there instead, on hooks in the cupboard or on the back of the door.

>> Bags

Who wants to be tripping over bags as soon as you get through the front door? A nightmare! Well, there's an easy way around it: a dedicated wall hook for each household member, or you can even hang them up high on a hat rack. Anything but clutter on the floor!

>> Other day-to-day items

Dog leads, umbrellas, shopping bags . . . the paraphernalia of daily life. All the stuff you take out regularly needs its own storage space. Slimline wall cabinets (the kind usually found in bathrooms) can work well in hallways – and if you can get hold of one with a mirror, or attach a mirror to the front, you've got a double-whammy hallway solution!

>> Seasonal items

It can be hard to call an official end to winter, with the British weather tending to warm up around February and then surprise you with some snow in March, but, even here in the UK, there are at least six months of the year when you definitely won't need a woolly bobble hat, scarf and mittens.

So, make sure you have somewhere away from the hallway to store that stuff in summer. Keep your precious hallway space free for what you really need every day.

>> Bikes, buggies and scooters

Believe me, I know . . . it's so tempting to wheel scooters, bikes and pushchairs into the hall and leave them there till the next day. We've all done it. But that means an evening of tripping over stuff and swearing on your way to the loo, and do you really want that?

OK, sometimes it's the only place to keep them. But instead, every time you come in, fold the pushchair down – it takes three seconds. And why not fix bike hooks onto the wall, to make sure bikes and scooters are off the floor and out of the way?

Hat racks: top rack
can store a box for
out-of-season items

Slimline cabinet usually found
in bathrooms to store small
items and provide a mirror

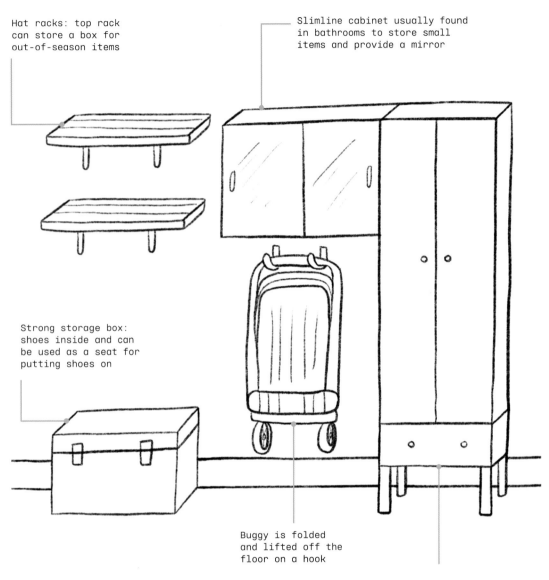

Strong storage box:
shoes inside and can
be used as a seat for
putting shoes on

Buggy is folded
and lifted off the
floor on a hook

Tall, slim
cupboard for
coats, umbrellas
and dog leads

YOUR IDEAL HALLWAY STORAGE SOLUTIONS

	NEEDED MOST DAYS	ALTERNATIVE HOME
KEYS	Yes, keep in hallway	——
SHOES	Some are. Keep 2-3 pairs per person in hall	Bottom of wardrobe; wellies in box in understairs cupboard
COATS	Yes, some. Keep 2 each in hallway	Put out-of-season coats in bedroom, clothes storage or box in loft
DOG ACCESSORIES	Yes, keep in hallway	——
UMBRELLAS	No, but need easy access, so keep in hallway	——
GLOVES, HATS, SCARVES	Seasonal need	Bedroom storage or box in loft out of season
BAGS	Yes, but only 1 each	Bedrooms for bags not currently in use
MAIL	Yes	Take through to kitchen to open and recycle junk mail
BIKES, SCOOTERS, BUGGIES	Yes	Outside – garden / shed / locked up in front of house

External Doors

We talked about the front of your front door at the start of this chapter, and there's more on that in the outdoor spaces chapter too, but what about the back of it? It's there in your hallway and it's just as important that it looks smart. I always paint the back of the door in the same colour as the hall walls. Don't fancy that? Fair enough – but just make sure you don't neglect it and leave it looking shabby! (For more on the front of your external doors, see page 238.)

DRAUGHTPROOFING

No one wants – or can afford – to spend more than they have to on fuel bills. Keeping the heat in and the cold air out is paramount!

On the most basic level, there is usually a draught through the gap between the door and the frame. Mind the gap, as they say on the Tube! It's crucial that you fill it, and in my time I've used anything that comes to hand as a quick fix: foil, polystyrene packaging, that foam stuff that protects picture frames . . . you name it! Basically, anything flexible that can fill the gaps and stay put.

Obviously, though, those aren't long-term solutions. Using proper draught-excluder tape is by far the best option. The other really simple thing you can do is to hang a heavyweight curtain across your hallway, just inside the front door. Old-fashioned? Maybe, but it can look great and it's super-effective at keeping the cold air out.

SECURITY

The most serious requirement of your front door – and of any external doors, come to that – is that they offer security against any of the many dodgy characters who might want to come in and have your stuff away.

I know it's not a very nice topic to think about, but criminals tend to go for the easiest targets, so don't let that be your gaff. Check your home insurance policy. There may be minimum requirements you need to meet for any claims to be valid.

Ideally your front door should have a mortise lock. These are the type that you need the key to open, as opposed to the single-barrel or Yale locks that can be opened from the inside by twisting a handle.

GLASS

Glass panels in front doors are great for letting in light, but they can also be a weak spot in the door. You can apply a special film to glass panels for extra protection. Check out your local DIY store or look online for options. Oh, and if you do have glass, make the most of it by cleaning it regularly! It's nice to see a sparkle in the mornings!

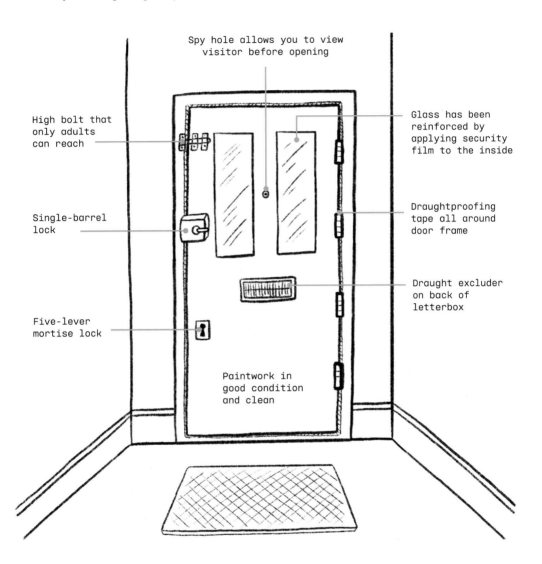

Spy hole allows you to view visitor before opening

High bolt that only adults can reach

Single-barrel lock

Five-lever mortise lock

Glass has been reinforced by applying security film to the inside

Draughtproofing tape all around door frame

Draught excluder on back of letterbox

Paintwork in good condition and clean

Jay's Top Tip *Got toddlers or dogs and need a stairgate? Well, I'm all for DIY, as you know, but when it comes to vital safety equipment like this, always use and install a proper stairgate that's been tested by the manufacturer. It's always best to leave safety items to the pros. I mean, you wouldn't knit your own seatbelt!*

My Favourite . . .

STAIRS STORAGE

You can get ideas for home décor everywhere. Inspiration is all around us, if we just remember to look. We all spend a lot of our time online nowadays and there are often good ideas to be found there.

Take Pinterest. For me, that site has so many pictures and suggestions that it can be overwhelming, but if you have the time and energy to go on a search, you'll find some cracking home-improvement ideas. And this one that I came across on there was a winner.

As I keep saying in this book, the one thing I hate in any room in the house is clutter. A messy home is a messy life, and I can't be doing with that! So, this plan to both create extra storage space AND clear up the hallway got my vote.

Until we grow wings, we all need stairs to get to another floor. The space under those first few stairs is almost always dead, wasted space – but it doesn't need to be. Why not think outside the box and build drawers inside your stairs?

As soon as I saw this idea, I was a man on a mission. I had access to the back of my stairway, so I built a supporting structure for the drawers then cut off the vertical backs of the steps with an electric saw.

It was surprisingly easy to fix drawers inside the steps and I fitted push magnets: the kind you get on the doors of kitchen units. As soon as I'd done that – wow! We had so much extra storage space! Shoes, slippers, kids' toys, knick-knacks . . . they all got stowed in there, and suddenly my hallway was immaculate – just how I like it! One thing to remember: always close the drawers, or you might come to mischief on the stairs at night in the dark! But, as long as you are careful with that, stair-drawers are a brilliant space-saver.

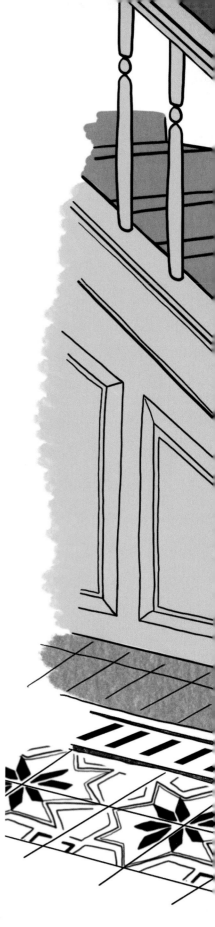

Bathroom

My basic preference for the bathroom is the same as for every other room in the house. I like everything to be streamlined, with no waste or clutter.

When you're designing and decorating any room in your house, take inspiration and ideas from everywhere. There's nothing wrong with copying cool looks that you have seen elsewhere, and when it comes to bathrooms in particular, I've taken so many great ideas from hotels.

Think about it, hotel owners have to dream up classy bathrooms that their guests love so much they want to come back and stay again and again. So why not make your own bathroom so slick and stylish that it's a joy for you to go into and get clean in every day?

I actually like a bathroom to look so cool that you almost feel as if you shouldn't be using it: that it's so immaculate it's as if you're disturbing perfection. Or maybe you are looking at your shower, thinking, I can't wait to get in there. It will lift me to another level!

My basic preference for the bathroom is the same as for every other room in the house. I like everything to be streamlined, with no waste or clutter. I don't even like bath mats! I'd rather have a cool wooden grille on the floor, like the ones you see in an upmarket hotel or in a sauna.

I've seen bathrooms I like that are painted, or even all done out with leather walls, but I prefer good old classic tiles, all day every day. I like them to be all white, with maybe four coloured tiles dotted in among them randomly, to pique people's interest: Huh? What are they doing there?

Then there's storage. You need a lot of stuff in bathrooms – shampoo, razors, toothbrushes, flannels, blah blah blah – but, personally, I can't be doing with old-fashioned wooden storage cabinets with steamed-up mirrors on the doors. Why not think a bit more inventively?

Along the full length of one of the tiled walls, my ideal bathroom would have an alcove shelf set a little way back in the wall for all the toiletries and bathroom nick-nacks. I'd have it deep enough and wide enough to store all of the towels in there, too, but I'll say more about this at the end of the chapter (see page 188).

I'll tell you one thing that I don't like in a bathroom – a bath! For me, it's all about showers. I might be weird, but I want to wash standing up. I mean, who wants to be sitting

I like bathrooms to be stylish, minimal and functional, because I grew up with ones that were the exact opposite.

in their own dirty water – yuck! Sorry, but it just doesn't do it for me. Budget permitting, I'd really love a wet room.

I absolutely love a power shower. I went to one hotel that had a copper showerhead the size of a frying pan, then smaller water jets all around me. I felt like I was in a car wash! It was wonderful, even if I did worry that my one single shower used more water than I'd normally need in a week.

It's worth going the extra mile because showers are important. I have ridiculously long showers. I don't sing in there (with my voice, I don't want to terrorize the neighbours!) but I do a lot of thinking. I gear up for the day in the mornings and I decompress at night.

I like bathrooms to be stylish, minimal and functional, because I grew up with ones that were the exact opposite. I remember so many no-nos: tiles with chicken patterns, stencils, toilet rolls hidden by crocheted dollies placed over the top. And don't get me started on soap-on-a-rope!

Having grown up on a council estate, I'm well used to living in flats and houses that didn't have separate bathrooms and toilets. When you needed to pee, you'd be banging on the bathroom door, cross-legged, with a big

question going round inside your head: shall I just go outside?

If you are lucky enough to have a separate little toilet room, what do you do with it, décor-wise? It's generally such a small space that it can be hard to leave your individual stamp on it, but I'd advise doing what you can to stop it just being a boring little cell-like enclosure.

Some people leave magazines by their loo, but I don't really like that, on the grounds of messiness and hygiene. A far quirkier solution can be to have newspaper articles or book pages pasted onto the wall. Who knows, they might spark an interesting conversation when you come out!

Another great thing I've seen in hotels is toilets where you don't even need to touch the loo! You wave your hand near a sensor and it opens or closes the lid, or even flushes it for you. It's amazing – peeing in the future! Why not try one in your home?

DIY in bathrooms comes with its own challenges. What are the dos and don'ts of tiling? How do you prevent leaks and keep water from where you really don't want it to go? And what are the best heating solutions? Here's how to bring hotel-style luxury to your humble home . . .

Getting *the* Best out *of* Existing Tiles

First off, you need to clean them – and I mean really, REALLY clean them! If you've ever dealt with tired tiling before you'll know that this isn't a quick job. But I'm going to give you some pointers to help you get that grout looking great and your tiles back in shape.

Think about exactly what you like and don't like about your existing tiles. There may be quick, low-budget fixes for you, depending on the specific issues you've got. We'll talk about tile paint on page 160, but before we go down that road, here are some other options to consider first.

SORT OUT YOUR GROTTY GROUT!

If your tiles need some TLC, I can pretty much guarantee that your grouting will need some sprucing up as well. So, let's start there!

Grout tends to get spots of mould on it over time and/or a yellowy-orange layer of . . . you know what? I'm not exactly sure what it is! What I do know is that seeing the back of that mess will immediately make your tiling look better.

Before you go out and buy a special tile cleaner, I recommend trying one of the following eco-friendly options first that you can easily make yourself. The simplest thing is good old washing up liquid – a good few squirts in a small bowl, topped up with warm water. swish together and get going with an old toothbrush dipped in the liquid. Or, mix a cup of bicarbonate of soda with enough water to make a paste. Apply this paste to your grout with an old toothbrush, leave it on for about half an hour then rinse off. Another great cleaner is white vinegar – spray it on and leave for about half an hour before rinsing off. It's no problem if it goes onto surrounding ceramic tiles, but if you have tiles made from anything else, check the manufacturer's guidance for cleaning products.

If any stubborn marks remain, give them a hard scrub with the old toothbrush and some more of your chosen cleaning agent, leave for half an hour, then rinse again. That should do it.

❯❯ Grout pens

If your grout is still looking a bit grotty, you can use a special type of paint that comes as a thick marker pen. You can match the colour to your grout – or even change the colour of your grout with it!

Now, you might be secretly tempted to skip the cleaning bit and go straight for this pen option, but take it from me: if you do that, it'll end in tears. The pen will look great at first, covering up the grime, but it won't last well – it just won't stick to dirt as well as it will to a clean surface. So put that elbow grease in first!

HOW TO CLEAN CERAMIC TILES

There is no shortage of brands of tile cleaner out there, and most of them are fine. At the same time, you can save your pennies and simply get the job done with white vinegar diluted 50:50 with water. If you want it to smell really good, add a few drops of lemon essential oil – the lemon has natural antibacterial properties as well, so it's a win–win.

Mix up some of your homemade tile-cleaning solution and put it in a spray bottle. You'll be thanking yourself later. You can get into all those nooks and crannies with a squirt in the right direction, and that old toothbrush will help you get rid of stubborn dirt. You'll soon be seeing your face in the tiles when you're done.

Jay's
Top Tip

Look online for other eco-friendly – and wallet-friendly – cleaning tips. Everyday ingredients such as vinegar, bicarb of soda and good old hot water can achieve amazing results and save you money.

CRACKED TILES?

Cracked tiles look pretty unsightly, and who wants to see that every morning in the shower? It's well worth a bit of effort to get the cracked ones out and put replacements in. Here's how you do it:

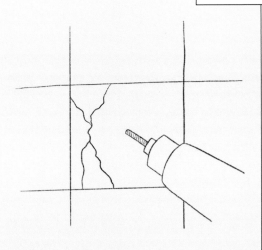

STEP 1

Drill a hole in the centre of each tile you want to remove. Wearing safety goggles, use a hammer and chisel to get behind the tile and ease it out. It'll usually break into several pieces.

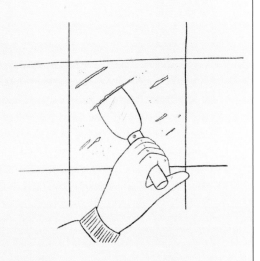

STEP 2

Once you've cleared all the bits of tile, carefully chisel out the old adhesive.

STEP 3

Spread the back of the new tile with tile adhesive. Be careful to put on just the right amount to ensure the new tile sits flush with the others. Press into place and wipe any excess from the surrounding tiles.

STEP 4

Once the adhesive has fully dried, grout around the new tile, wiping any excess or grouting that gets on the tile. There you go. Problem solved!

Tile Paint

Back in the day, people routinely used gloss paint on tiles to perk them up. This didn't yield very impressive or long-lasting results. But I've got great news: modern tile paint is really good, and it's a quick, cheap and easy way to revamp your bathroom. As with everything, the absolute key to success is to prepare well. First, remove all traces of dirt, grease and grime from your tiles. Check the recommendations on your paint tin for guidance, then apply the paint with a brush or a small roller.

Remember: the grout will be painted, too. So, if there's any damage to repair, for example filling in missing bits, get that sorted out, then sand the tile smooth and wipe away any dust. Also, leave plenty of drying time before you start prepping to paint.

PREPARING TO PAINT

Follow all of the tips on pages 154–159 about cleaning your tiles. Check they're properly 'squeaky clean'. Use a fine sandpaper to lightly sand the surface, which will give the best foundation for your tile paint to stick to. Once that's done, wash them down again with sugar soap or warm soapy water to remove the dust. Next on the to-do list: tape all of the edges so your tile paint stays on the tiles and doesn't escape to any other areas. Decorator's tape or masking tape is your friend here. Don't rush it: take your time and apply it carefully and accurately. Don't forget to cover your bath, shower tray and flooring if you've got tile paint anywhere near them, or you might be getting some unsightly bathroom splashes!

Jay's Top Tip

Don't forget to cover your bath, shower tray and flooring if you've got tile paint anywhere near them, or you might be getting some unsightly bathroom splashes!

APPLYING THE PAINT

I'll keep saying this until I'm blue in the face, like a Smurf: read the instructions on the tin! With any tile paint, the best finish is going to be achieved via even, gentle strokes of a good-quality paintbrush, or the smooth movements of a roller while you apply even pressure. Apply small amounts of paint at a time, covering a specific area, and move across the tiled surface methodically. If you come across a bit where the paint doesn't want to stick, don't just keep going over and over it – that ain't going to work! Instead, use a damp cloth to remove the paint from that tile, then give it a scrub with a scouring pad dipped in soapy water or sugar soap. Wipe dry with a lint-free cloth and you're ready to carry on painting.

One coat should be enough. However, if you're painting in a colour that's very different in tone from the tiles underneath (i.e. dark paint on pale tiles, or pale paint on dark tiles) or your tiles have a pattern on them, you may need a second coat. Always check your paint tin for recommended drying times between coats.

REMOVING OLD TILE PAINT

If you've moved into a place with a dodgy tile-paint job, or one that was done so long ago that it needs a bit of TLC, the best thing to do is to strip it all off and assess the tiles underneath. There's no way of knowing what you'll find, but you might be pleasantly surprised and find tiles underneath that are in good condition that you like. Stripping off tile paint is usually pretty easy. If there is any chance that the paint is decades old and could contain lead, test it first using a proper testing kit. And if the paint does contain lead, it's vital that you seek professional advice about disposing of it (see page 59).

- **SCRAPING METHOD**: This method is exactly what it sounds like. Use a sharp paint scraper or utility knife to gently but firmly scrape away the old paint. If it only comes away in small flakes and seems stubborn to shift, take your hat off to whoever first applied it! They did a good job, but it means you'll need to make use of either heat or a chemical stripper.

- **HEATING METHOD**: Using a heat gun helps soften the paint enough to scrape it off in bigger sections. Follow the instructions on your heat gun and be careful to keep it moving over the paint so you don't scorch particular spots and damage the tiles. Once the paint over a smallish area (say about 30cm square) feels tacky and soft, get scraping and it should lift off easily.

- **PAINT STRIPPER METHOD**: Are you wrinkling up your nose at the thought of all those eye-watering chemicals? I don't blame you, but you'll be pleased to know that paint strippers have moved on in the last few decades. They're much less hazardous and nicer to use now. Shop around and you should be able to find a good water-based stripper. These are non-toxic and don't give off harmful fumes, but they do the job well. Apply the gel or paste to the paint, then leave it to work its magic for the time recommended by the manufacturer. After that, either scrape or scrub it off, again following whatever instructions are on the packet.

Tiling Walls

If you've got the right equipment, decent tools and – the important bit – a love of straight lines, this is a very satisfying job for you. No, trust me, it really is!

Tiles absolutely transform a bathroom (or any room, but bathrooms and kitchens are the usual favourites). So, plan carefully, get all the stages clear in your mind, and allow enough time to do all the work.

Remember: factor in drying time for the tile adhesive, and bear in mind that cutting tiles around awkward obstacles can be fiddly.

HOW MANY TILES?

Once you've decided where your tiles will go, measure the area that needs to be covered.

It's very likely you'll be tiling more than one wall, so tackle each section separately. It's mathematics time: measure the height and the width, multiply them together, and that gives your area. See opposite for an example.

Remember to add a further 10 per cent when you're buying the tiles to allow for inevitable breakages and, if you can, try to buy tiles with the same batch number on the box for a perfect colour match.

Jay's Top Tip

If you're tiling a space that isn't rectangular or square, sketch it out and divide it into squares or rectangles. Then – calculators out! – you can calculate the area of the separate parts and add them together to find the total area.

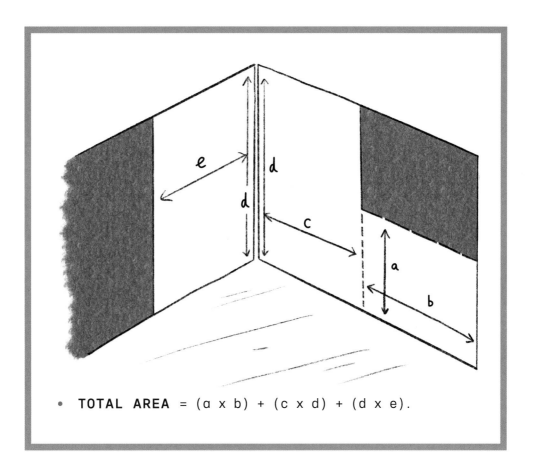

- **TOTAL AREA** = (a x b) + (c x d) + (d x e).

TILING OVER EXISTING TILES

I know – this sounds a right bodge-job! But, believe me, it's not. It's a respected method of re-doing your tiles, as long as the ones you're covering up are in good condition and not loose, and the surfaces are smooth and flat with no bowing.

Taking tiles off a wall if they're firmly in place is proper hard work. It can also damage the plaster on the wall underneath. So, for the sake of losing a couple of centimetres from the size of your bathroom, why not just tile over the top? You'll be amazed at how well it works.

The crucial thing to remember if you're tiling over existing tiles is to offset the new ones so that the grouting lines don't match up. Follow the advice on page 164 about how to position your tiles, but then shift the first one to the left, right, up or down to avoid aligning the joins with those underneath.

TILE POSITIONING

It's unlikely that your walls are absolutely straight or have dimensions that mean that your chosen tiles will fit the space perfectly. If that does happen, wow, you must have been stroking a lot of black cats recently!

However, assuming that you're not the luckiest person in the DIY world, you'll need to think carefully about where to place your tiles so that the cut ones at the edges of the wall are all roughly the same width and not too thin. The last thing you want is to be trying to cut thin slivers of tile, because that is a nightmare.

So, where to put that all-important first tile? Maths time again: the best way to work it out is to measure the width of the wall to be tiled, then divide that figure by your tile width plus the size of your tile spacers.

Let's say your wall is 2.4m wide and you are using 15cm tiles with 2mm spacers. Let's convert all that into millimetres: 2400mm, 150mm and 2mm. Use a calculator to find out 2,400 divided by 152: the answer is 15.789.

So, rounding up, you'll need 15 whole tiles plus 0.8 tiles for one row across your wall. Or, if you centre the whole tile section, you'd have 15 tiles with 0.4 tiles at each end. This will look great and you won't have those dreaded tiny slivers of tile to deal with. Happy days!

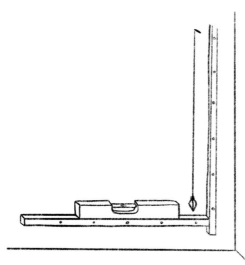

PERFECTLY STRAIGHT

You need your tiles to be absolutely straight. The best way to ensure this is to use a batten and a level to establish a perfectly horizontal line for the first row of tiles that you'll stick down.

Usually, you'll place the batten one-tile-height up from the floor, measured at the lowest point of the floor if it isn't level. Using a second batten perfectly perpendicular to your horizontal one makes sure your first vertical column will be aligned correctly. Don't worry – it's easier than it sounds!

STICKING THE TILES TO THE WALL

This is really straightforward so long as you've got the right adhesive and the right tools. Make sure you but the right tile adhesive for your tiles, and always ready the instructions on the tub. Got your notched spreader at the ready? Here we go!

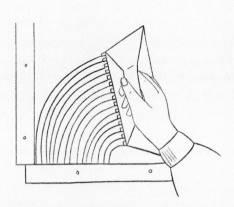

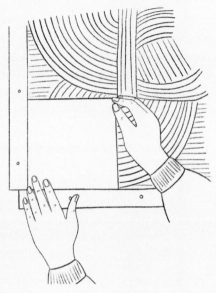

STEP 1

Spread tile adhesive onto the wall
with a trowel. Begin at the place where
your two battens meet. Work upwards
and outwards to cover up to one square
metre. Use a notched spreader to even
out the depth of the adhesive and
create grooves to help the tiles stick.

STEP 2

Place your first tile in the corner where
the battens meet. Press it down firmly
and evenly.

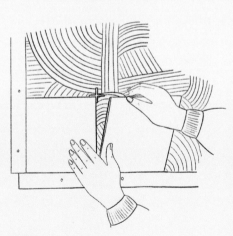

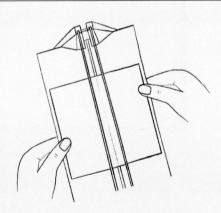

STEP 3

Insert tile s pacers to the side of the
first tile. Place the second tile to
butt up to the spacers and the batten.
Carry on like this until the area to be
covered with whole tiles is complete.

STEP 4

Once the adhesive has dried (usually
about twelve hours, but check the
instructions on the packaging), remove
the battens and cut tiles to fit around
the edges. Stick them with adhesive
spread on the back of each tile with the
notched spreader if it's easier. Leave
to dry completely.

CUTTING TILES TO FIT

This all starts with accurate measuring! Remember: the size of tile you need at the top of the wall may not be exactly the same as the size at the bottom, so measuring for each one is the surest way to achieve a good finish.

You can use a tape measure to measure the gap at the top and bottom of each tile, then subtract the width of your tile spacers. Or you can use the same method as I explained for the soft floor tiles on page 62. Either will work, so do whichever you feel comfortable with.

- **CUTTING STRAIGHT LINES**: The best tool for this is a platform tile cutter. They score a line in the glazed (upper) side of the tile so you can snap the tile along the score line cleanly and accurately.

- **CUTTING A SLIVER OFF A TILE**: Score the glazed side of the tile at the correct position, using a tile cutter or a steel rule and utility knife. Make sure to score right through the glaze or you risk not getting a clean edge. Use tile nippers to 'nibble' off the sliver, then sand the edge of the tile for a smooth finish, if needed. Do this carefully and it will look great.

- **CUTTING CURVES**: To cut curves, you'll need a tile saw. It has a blade that's more like a thin, rough, tensioned wire. Mark the shape to be cut onto the tile, then clamp it to a workbench with an offcut of board or wood on top of the glazed side to protect it. Saw around the shape.

TILING ROUND CORNERS

You and I know that the chances are you're not just tiling on one wall of your bathroom. So, you'll need to know what to do at the corners. Have no fear, the simple answer is . . . it's simple!

All you need to do is take it one wall at a time. Tile your first wall right up to the edges. Then tile your second wall with the tiles at the edge butting up to the face of the tiles on wall one. Easy-peasy!

'But Jay!' I hear you cry. 'How do I make sure my lines all match up?'

Well, battens and a level are your friends here again. In fact, nailing battens in place on your second (and third, and fourth!) wall at the same time as the first is a smart move. You can check everything is level, and lining up, before opening that tub of adhesive.

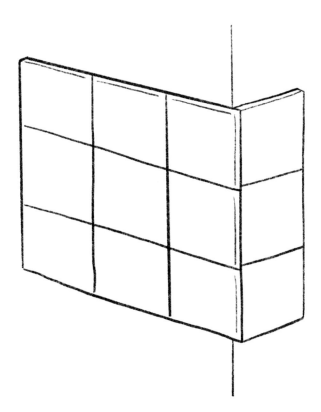

GROUTING

Here's what you've been waiting for – the 'Ta-da!' moment when all of your careful prep and hard work pays off. Once the tile adhesive is dry, remove your tile spacers. They can be reused, so save them for another tiling project.

Now, this is fairly obvious, but I'm going to say it anyway: make sure you buy the right sort of grout. For bathrooms, you'll need waterproof grout, even if you're not tiling the shower or the area beside the bath. In a kitchen or other space, standard grout should be OK unless, you think there'll be a lot of water splashing onto your tiles for some reason.

Make sure there's no adhesive stuck to your tiles. Give them a good wipe down and remove any stray splats with a scraper. Wipe your tiles with a damp cloth and, once they are all looking cushty and dry, it's grouting time!

Use a small sponge or grout float to wipe the grout over the tiled surface, pressing it into the cracks. Wipe away the surplus with a clean, damp sponge. Carry on until all the cracks are filled. And there you are. Take a bow, because it will look amazing!

TILING FLOORS

The same logic for tiling walls applies to floors. However, there are a few extra things to take into consideration.

Floor tiles tend to be bigger than wall tiles. This means it's even more important to consider where the joins run. For example, centring a row of tiles in the doorway will likely look a lot better than having an offset join line catching your eye as you walk into the room.

Also think about how your feet will feel in winter on ceramic tiles. The answer is pretty cold, unless you're installing underfloor heating! This used to be the preserve of the very rich and luxury hotels in the past, but it has become a lot more affordable in recent years. The electric type in particular won't even add much height to your floor. It's well worth thinking of as an option.

Bathroom Flooring

Tiles? Vinyl? Painted floorboards? Luxury vinyl tiles? Linoleum? Choices, choices – but which one are you going to go for?

Well, firstly, have a good think about what will work practically for you and your family. It may be that you simply need to make the most of what you've got, especially if you're renting, and I've got good tips on that on page 172.

However, if you're doing a more full-on renovation, it might be a chance to make a change. Look at the different properties of each flooring type to help you come to a decision, and think about how they'll look in your bathroom.

Oh, and a word on colour: dark flooring in bathrooms tends to show up ALL the dust, while very pale flooring can get grubby pretty fast. So, unless you don't mind some mess or you really like cleaning, opt for mid-tone shades.

Jay's
Top Tip

Make sure that the feet of any bathroom furniture won't mark the tiles.

	PROS	CONS
NATURAL WOODEN FLOORBOARDS	Warm underfoot, budget-friendly	Can easily become water-damaged, even with varnish or oiling
ENGINEERED WOOD BOARDS	Warm underfoot, less prone to water damage than natural wood	Need any sawn edges properly sealing; can be slippery when wet depending on finish
CERAMIC TILES	Huge range of colours and patterns available; easy to clean; waterproof	Can be cold underfoot, some can be slippery when wet, very hard surface
LUXURY VINYL TILES	Large range of colours and styles; easy to install; warm underfoot; hardwearing	Relatively expensive; not very eco-friendly
SHEET VINYL	Very budget-friendly; easy to lay; massive range of patterns and colours	Not eco-friendly; needs perfectly flat and smooth sub-floor
CUSHIONED SHEET VINYL	Budget-friendly; easy to lay; good for slightly uneven surfaces; soft and warm underfoot	Not eco-friendly; can wear out in high-traffic areas
LINOLEUM	Eco-friendly; large range of colours; warm underfoot; extremely hardwearing	Relatively expensive; not as easy to lay as vinyl

Jay's Top Tip

If your floor is in any way 'springy' or has any big dips in it, get the sub-floor checked out by a professional. If there's been past water damage, there could be rotten floor joists. That's a problem that needs urgent attention.

CLEANING BATHROOM FLOORS

There's a special sort of dusty grime that tends to build up on bathroom floors. Sometimes the only way to really get rid of it is with a scrubbing brush and some elbow grease. And if you live in a hard-water area (the test: limescale build-up inside your kettle? Then you definitely do!), you'll probably have water marks to remove as well from areas that get regular splashes or drips.

How to do it is proper old-school. Reach for that trusty toothbrush again, run a bowl of warm, soapy water, start in one corner of the floor and scrub, scrub, scrub. Use a bigger scrubbing brush or a gentle abrasive pad for the main areas, and keep slogging away until the whole floor is done. You'll probably need a damp cloth to wipe up the dirty suds, and a change of water halfway through.

If you still have water marks after all that palaver, there are limescale removers you can use. Alternatively, try white vinegar or lemon juice (as long as your flooring isn't made from anything porous, such as stone or marble).

Once you've got a properly clean floor, make yourself a cuppa – you've earned it! Then take a look around you. You're now in a position to assess whether your floor needs a bit of work – or completely replacing.

›› Fixing scratches

If your flooring has ugly scratches, you can probably make it look loads better even if you can't get rid of the marks completely.

For any surface that's got a plasticky or vinyl top layer, gently rub down the scratch with really fine-grit sandpaper, then apply an oily or waxy furniture polish and buff it up with a soft lint-free cloth. You should see a big improvement straight away.

For scratches in natural wood, get your nuts out! Rubbing a walnut over the scratch should work well for darker wood. You can also buy wax-repair sticks in different natural shades to match your boards.

For ceramic tiles, I'd advise talking to your local hardware or tile store. There are lots of repair kits out there, but it's important to get the right one for your particular tiles.

Jay's Top Tip

Once your floor is totally clean, you might notice the skirting boards looking a bit the worse for wear. A good clean might be all they need, too, but see pages 93 and 124 for more info.

LAYING VINYL FLOORING

You'll be glad to learn that this is a relatively easy job to do yourself, and as such offers a very cost-effective way to redo your bathroom floor to give a hard-wearing, practical finish with tons of colour options.

The vinyl comes on a big roll, like carpet, and you can cut it to fit your space perfectly with good scissors and a sharp utility knife. If you can't avoid joins, plan them carefully and you can achieve a seamless look worthy of any pro.

Step *by* Step

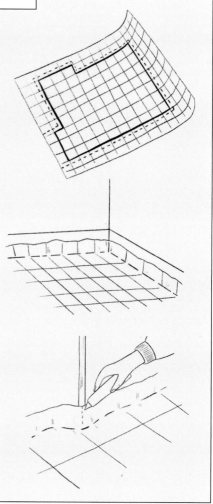

STEP 1

Clear the biggest area you can in a room close to your bathroom and unroll the sheet vinyl. Referring to your measurement diagram, roughly mark out the outline of the floor space, then measure and mark an additional 10cm all the way around. Cut the vinyl on these outer marks.

STEP 2

Place the piece of vinyl in your bathroom, positioning it carefully on the floor and smoothing it into place, with the excess running up the walls. Make sure any pattern looks straight from the doorway looking into the room – this is where you will notice if it's a bit squiffy. Realign as needed. Let the flooring rest in place for a few hours.

STEP 3

Where there are obstacles to cut around, such as pipes, make a vertical cut from the edge of the sheet to the obstacle. Then cut small notches to allow the vinyl to lie flat around the pipe and trim off the excess.

You'll need to plan the best way to lay the flooring, especially if you have a directional pattern. Once you know the width of vinyl you need, sketch out a plan of your bathroom floor (and decide where any joins will go, if you can't avoid them).

Remember to factor in some wastage for matching patterns – oh, and always round up from the required length when making your order. Trust me, it's better to have 20cm of spare vinyl than a 2cm gap at one end!

Prepare the floor as you would for laying solid wood flooring (see page 60), making sure it's clean and level, and removing the threshold strip first if there's one in your doorway.

Step *by* Step

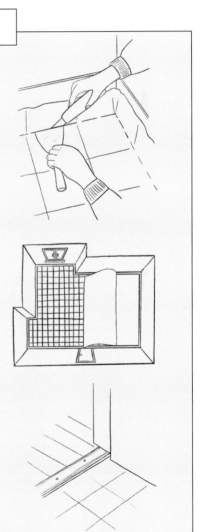

STEP 4

Pushing the vinyl firmly up to the edge of the floor, trim off the excess with a utility knife held at 45 degrees to the floor. Make sure that its point is pushing into the right angle where floor meets wall.

STEP 5

Once the vinyl is all cut and fits perfectly, it's time to get sticking! Gently pull up one side of the vinyl and fold it back towards the centre of the room, exposing about half the floor underneath. Apply adhesive to that half of the floor as per the manufacturer's instructions, then carefully unfold the vinyl and push it down into the adhesive. Use a soft broom to smooth it from the centre out towards the edges.

STEP 6

Repeat step 5 for the other half of the vinyl. Once the adhesive has dried, finish off the edges of the floor using caulk or mastic (see pages 176–177), and replace (or add) the threshold strip at the doorway.

Keeping *the* Water Out

It's crucial that you make certain areas of your bathroom watertight. This will prevent water seeping into walls, under flooring or down the side of the basin, shower or bath. If you don't, all your hard DIY work will be rapidly undone and water will get into the fabric of your home and cause havoc.

The best way to do this is to finish the joins between different elements with silicone sealant. Unlike normal decorator's caulk, silicone sealant is super-flexible and sticks like glue to all surfaces it touches. You can't paint over it to suit your design, but it does come in a range of different colours.

SILICONE SEALANT VS DECORATOR'S CAULK

Which product to use for which job? Both come in similar tubes with long nozzles and are applied using a caulking gun, but it's really important you don't get them mixed up!

Decorator's caulk is used for neatly filling the joins between different surfaces, such as where a doorframe or skirting board meets a wall. It's fairly solid when it dries and you can paint over it, which is useful. However, it doesn't stick to surfaces all that firmly and it won't keep water out for long, so it's best avoided anywhere in the bathroom that water could splash. Which, let's face it, is pretty much everywhere.

Silicon sealant is very flexible and sticks to any surface it's applied to. Once dry, it has a shiny finish and nothing sticks to it – not even paint. Its job is to create a watertight seal between different surfaces, and if applied correctly, it lasts for years. So, there's our winner for the bathroom!

GETTING RID OF BLACK MOULD FROM SEALANT

Black spots on your sealant is not a good look, and neither is it very healthy for your family to be around. The good news is that it's removable with a bit of time and patience. You can buy special cleaners for this purpose, or use a couple of simple household products. The most eco-friendly approach is to use a paste made from white vinegar and bicarbonate of soda. Wearing rubber gloves, apply it to the spotty sealant and leave for twenty-four hours. Rinse off and you should see good results. If there is still some mould showing, do it again.

The other effective mould-killer is thickened household bleach. Bear in mind, you must wear rubber gloves for this. Again, it needs to stay in place on the sealant for twelve to twenty-four hours. Best is to apply the bleach then push screwed-up lengths of toilet paper against it, pressing it into the line of sealant, and applying more bleach if needed. When it's all sorted, make sure you dispose of the paper carefully and rinse off all the bleach remnants.

REMOVING OLD SEALANT

Here's how to get rid of unwanted old sealant. With a sharp utility knife or sealant-remover tool, first cut away as much of the sealant as you can without damaging the surfaces it's stuck to.

Once you've removed the bulk of it, you'll need some help to get the final bits off. You can buy silicone sealant remover, but if you have some WD-40 in the house, and some denatured alcohol (methylated spirit), you can use that instead. Spray on the WD-40 and leave it for about twenty minutes. The last bits of sealant should just lift off. You'll then need to wipe down the sprayed area with a cloth soaked in denatured alcohol to remove the WD-40 residue. Job done!

HOW TO APPLY SILICONE SEALANT

First, make sure the surfaces are clean, dry and free from any dust or grease. If you haven't used a caulk gun before, have a practice on some waste materials or an old cardboard box. The trick is to get a nice even flow of sealant so you can control the bead of silicone and get a smooth line. It's quite addictive, once you get going! (Or is that just me?)

As always, read the instructions on the product before you start. And make sure you open a window – the sealant gives off fumes as it cures.

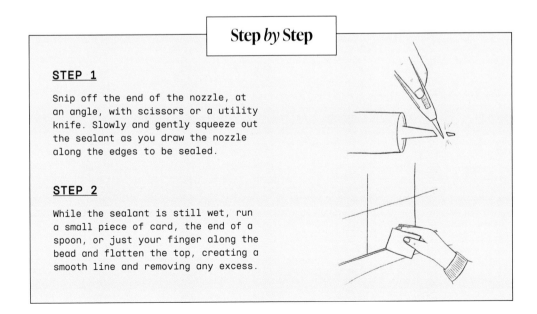

Step *by* Step

STEP 1

Snip off the end of the nozzle, at an angle, with scissors or a utility knife. Slowly and gently squeeze out the sealant as you draw the nozzle along the edges to be sealed.

STEP 2

While the sealant is still wet, run a small piece of card, the end of a spoon, or just your finger along the bead and flatten the top, creating a smooth line and removing any excess.

Fixing Common Plumbing Issues

We all need plumbers, and there are plenty of jobs you should definitely leave to the professionals. However, with a bit of know-how and being savvy about how the basics work, you can sort out a few simple plumbing issues yourself.

It's vital to know how to shut off the water for your entire house, in case you ever need to. Make sure you know where your stopcock is and that you can get to it easily. Tell all of the other members of your household where it is as well!

WATER IN UNEXPECTED PLACES

If you notice water somewhere unexpected – and unwanted – in your bathroom, the chances are you've got a small leak from a pipe, radiator or valve. Oh, great! So how do you fix it?

First things first. Mop up the water and find out where it came from, then set a bowl or tray in place to catch any further drips. The last thing you need is water damage! Then ask yourself a few sensible questions:

1 **IS THE LEAK COMING FROM A VALVE OR ANYWHERE WITH NUTS THAT CAN BE TIGHTENED?** If so, try tightening them and see if it fixes the issue.

2 **IS THE LEAK COMING FROM A WASTE PIPE?** If it's anywhere near your U-bend, bottle trap or S-bend, you may have a partial blockage that means water is sitting around the pipe joins for longer than it should. See page 180 for advice on clearing blockages.

3 **IS THE PROBLEM COMING FROM WHERE ONE PIPE SCREWS ONTO ANOTHER?** Tighten up the screw joint and apply PTFE tape onto the thread of the joint before screwing on the other side. It forms a really watertight seal.

CLEARING BLOCKAGES

OK, I've got to warn you, this won't be pretty. In fact, this job can be revolting if it's not been done for a while. Basically, hair, soap scum, toothpaste, shampoo and conditioner all love to hang around in your pipes, clinging to the sides and gathering more recruits for their gunk-and-slime party as the days and weeks go by. Yuck!

The easiest way to access your waste pipes is by removing the U-bend or bottle trap. It should be obvious how to unscrew them as they are designed to be removed easily. But remember: there's water in there! Put a big bucket underneath before you start unscrewing.

Once your trap is free, use an old cloth or some kitchen towel to wipe out the gunk. Remember not to rinse it in the sink or bath you've just removed it from – your waste pipe has a bit missing! Clear any visible slimy bits from the pipes with that trusty old toothbrush or a washing-up brush.

Before you replace the trap, check the edges of the pipes for damage. Are any rubber washers on push-fit fittings in good condition and in the right place? Are the parts to be re-joined all clean and dry? Double-check them: you can't be too sure. If you should need to replace any components, remember to take the old one with you to your DIY store and match it to a new part.

THE DRIPPING TAP

You know what? If we were going to give out prizes for the most common bathroom problem, I reckon this would be the winner. By a long way!

And yet dripping taps are super easy to fix. Usually, all you need to do is replace the rubber washers inside. It's a job you can easily do yourself, as long as your taps are standard.

First, shut off the water to the taps. Most pipes leading to taps have a special valve so that you can stop the water reaching just that tap and the rest of your house is unaffected. The valves look a bit like this, and all you need to do is turn the screw with a screwdriver:

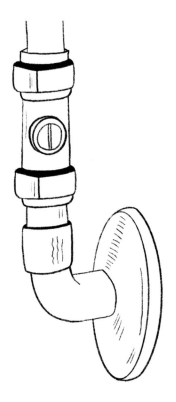

Now, have a butcher's at your tap. With nearly all of them, you can just take the tap apart, remove the degraded washers, replace them with new ones, and put it back together. Easy, right?

Well, up to a point! I'm very aware that some 'easy' tasks can end up taking all day and lead to you filling up the swear jar! However, there are a few tips and hacks to help you get the job done.

Look at this diagram of a standard tap and see how its different components fit together:

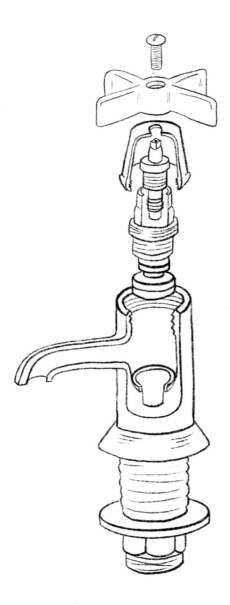

This may not be exactly identical to your tap. However, you should be able to see on your tap, probably at the back or on top, a point where you can begin to take it apart. On this diagram, it would be the grub screw at the top, after flipping off its little cap.

TAKING YOUR OWN TAP APART

- Put the plug into the plughole so you don't lose any pieces.

- Have your phone at the ready to take photos of what fits where as you take it apart. This will help you with reassembly.

- Put a paper towel or cloth on the side of the sink to place each part onto. Important: place them in order of removal.

- Work methodically and slowly, and never force a component out as it could break.

- Don't panic!

When you've taken your tap to bits, you'll have at least one rubber washer. Replace it and any others with new ones, and inspect the other elements of the tap. If anything looks worn or cracked, you might be able to order just that component rather than replace the whole tap, which can be a cheaper option. Your handy local DIY store can advise you on this if you show them the problem part. Or you might be able to find the part online. It helps to know the brand and/or model of the tap before you start your search.

When it comes to putting everything back together, make sure that all parts are clean and dry, then reverse the process for taking the tap apart. You're now a DIY plumber and you deserve another nice cuppa. Maybe even a biscuit!

Jay's Top Tip

If you are in any doubt about taking your tap apart and putting it together again, there's no shame in getting some help! Some people love doing this sort of puzzle, but it's not for everyone! There are many different aspects of DIY, and just because you enjoy one sort of task doesn't mean you ought to like them all.

The Toilet

Let's talk toilets! Nobody except primary school kids likes to talk about loos and poos very much but, let's face it, your toilet is the most important seat in the house!

Everyone wants their toilet to be clean and functional, and it also helps if it's safe to sit on. Who wants a wobbly loo seat? A dodgy flush action is another no-no. You don't want to make embarrassed visitors have to tell you that they can't make your lavatory flush.

And while we're talking toilets, I've got a personal bugbear: toilet-brush holders that are open at the top. It's fine if the loo brush is clean, but if it's not, you might be seeing sights that put you off your dinner!

Yuck! Moving quickly on . . .

SPRING-CLEANING THE THRONE

Before you do anything to your toilet, it's essential to give it a thorough clean. Use a loo brush for inside the bowl and under the rim, and a cloth and another old toothbrush for the outer parts. You'll also need toilet cleaner and some hot soapy water.

First things first: start by flushing the loo. Squirt the cleaner under the rim and let it sit there as you clean the rest of the toilet. Use hot soapy water, plus get to work with the toothbrush to scrub away any grime in and around the joints where the seat is attached.

Don't forget to wipe the whole of the outside of the bowl, right down to the floor. At the very least, there is likely to be dust. There may also be other marks, but let's not talk about those, eh?

When the toilet body, seat and lid are looking clean, get that loo brush and have a good scrub under the rim and inside the bowl. Pay special attention to the bit where the water line is. One final flush and your loo should be gleaming!

FIXING OR REPLACING A WOBBLY SEAT

A word on toilet design. You'll see two holes in them, on the top, behind the bowl. Their function is simple: this is where the toilet seat attaches.

Now, these holes can be in different positions, depending on the style of your toilet. This means that manufacturers have to leave some flexibility in their fixings – which, obviously, means that there are parts that can work loose.

If you and your loved ones are wobbling about while you're trying to do your toilet business, you can solve this by tightening the wing nuts or hexagonal nuts holding the seat in place. If that doesn't fix the issue, you'll need to undo those nuts and take the seat off completely.

Have a look at what's going on with the hinges. Has the adjustable element come loose? Can you tighten it? If something has snapped or corroded, can you replace or fix it? You may be able to buy new fixings and keep the seat. If you can't, it's time for a new seat.

Before you go loo-seat shopping, measure the distance between the holes in your toilet where the seat fixings go; the length from the front of the bowl to the back, parallel to the holes; and the width at the widest part of the bowl.

Now, off to the DIY store, where you can use these measurements to find a seat that will fit your loo. Happy flushing!

Bathroom Lighting

I'm really not a fan of bright lighting anywhere in the home. Having said that, you do need decent illumination in the bathroom so that you can shave or put on make-up without having to guess where your face is.

Ideally, I like to have more than one lighting option. A good way to do this is to have a main room light that isn't too bright and complement this with a small light specifically for your mirror above the basin. That way, you can do your morning and evening ablutions in comfort without feeling like you're under floodlights.

SAFE LIGHTING

As bathrooms tend to get quite steamy, it's important that you only ever use light fittings that are specifically designed for these environments. These fittings will have some sort of housing that stops moisture from getting close to the bulb.

We all know that water and electricity aren't a good mix, but you do still have some options in terms of changing the mood. Opt for bulbs that are less bright, or change them to 'warm white' for a cosier, more welcoming vibe.

I'm a big fan of candles, and lighting candles in the bathroom while you're having a bath or shower is a great way to chill out after a long day. Boring but necessary safety note: make sure that naked flames aren't close to anything that could catch fire.

PULL-CORDS

Bathrooms often have pull-cord light switches instead of wall switches because they are safer, with less risk of getting an electrical shock. However, they aren't built to last forever, and they do need cleaning. You can change the cord-end pretty easily by sliding the old one up the cord, undoing the knot (or trimming it off), removing the cord-end, then threading the cord into a new end and re-knotting.

If the pull-cord is looking a bit grubby, it's time to wash it or replace it. This shouldn't involve taking the actual fitting apart. However, if you find you do you need to do that, ask a qualified electrician. They'll be able to test the wiring once the job is done and check everything is in order.

My Favourite...

BATHROOM STORAGE

This little feature is a bit different from the other favourites I describe in this book, because I've never actually done it! All I've managed to do so far is fantasize about it. But I can visualize exactly how it will look, and I know that I am 100 per cent going to do it one day. Bathrooms are functional rooms, and if you're not careful they can be boring. It can be difficult to see beyond the usual basic arrangement of bath/shower/toilet/sink/bathroom cabinet – until you start thinking outside the box.

My major concern in bathrooms is storage. I don't like seeing shampoos, soaps and toothbrushes lying about on the basin and littering the place up, but I'm not a big fan of keeping absolutely everything in bathroom cabinets either. So... why not keep all of your everyday bits and bobs in a smart alcove?

What I want is a recess, one that's about 30–40cm high and 20–30cm deep, running the length of one wall and functioning as a shelf. I'll build it fairly high, so it runs above the toilet, through the shower area, but passes under the mirror where I shave. And it needs to be deep enough to hold folded or rolled towels, too.

This alcove shelf will hold everything that's used regularly: creams, ointments, shampoo, toilet rolls, towels, the works. I'm making this cubby hole sound like a dumping ground – but it won't be! There'll be no multi-sized, multi-coloured toiletries, because I like to decant everything into brown glass bottles with pump dispensers. As well as being ultra-practical, they look totally amazing!

Ah, Jay's ideal bathroom! I'm grinning even thinking about it! Now, all that I have to do is actually build the thing...

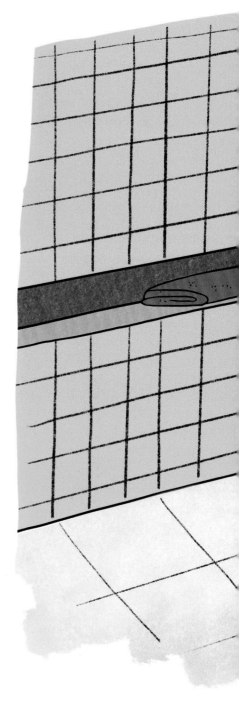

Bedroom

Your bedroom is such a major room. It's where you start your day when you wake up every morning, and where you end it when you lay down to sleep at night.

When we talked about bathrooms in the previous chapter, I advised you to take some inspiration from hotel bathrooms. That is the last thing you should do for your bedroom. Hotel bedrooms are pretty boring; you get a bed, a bedside table, a wardrobe, a chair, a TV and . . . bosh!

That's it! Well, I believe that's just not good enough; bedrooms need a lot more imagination, individuality, life – and soul – than that. Your bedroom is such a major room. It's where you start your day when you wake up, and where you end it when you lay down to sleep. These are two very personal, important moments, so who would want to spend them in a room that they don't love?

For me, the most important quality for any bedroom – and this may not even be a word, but if it isn't, it should be – is comfortability. Even if the rest of your house is minimal and functional, like mine pretty much is, the bedroom should be all about ease and luxury. About comfortability.

When it comes to décor and fitting out the bedroom, I spend more on it than any other room in the house. I'm not afraid to go to town. Yet that doesn't just mean shelling out for top-of-the-range stuff. The most important item in the room is the bed – and I normally build it myself. I always have done. When I had no dosh, I'd get hold of a few pallets (don't ask how!), stack them together and put a mattress on top.

Nowadays, I'm more likely to make the frame, legs and slats from decent timber and use a lovely old wardrobe door for a headboard (see page 230).

That's a pretty cheap job to do, but I won't then skimp on the bedding. I love a superking-size bed – I'm a tall geezer, and I don't want my feet hanging off the end and getting cold! I'll get nice cotton sheets and a brushed cotton duvet, loads of luxurious pillows and, if I've got it, I'll happily spend four figures on a mattress. It's worth it to have a blissful kip every night.

The bedroom is the one room in the house where I definitely want carpet. The thicker the better! I'll even go as far as a nice eighties-style shag pile. I'd much rather get out of bed and sink into that than have to scrabble around on a cold floor for my slippers.

When it comes to bedroom storage, I'm all about walk-in closets. I've often upcycled old kitchen cupboards into storage units within walk-in closets

Because I dislike conventional, hotel-style bedrooms, I like to do something different for bedside cabinets. I've used glass shelves before, and in one house I hung baskets from the ceiling to float next to the bed. Try it! The only limit is your imagination.

When it comes to bedroom storage, I'm all about walk-in closets. I've often upcycled old kitchen cupboards into storage units within walk-in closets. In one house we had a spare bedroom, and I got some rails and MDF and basically turned the whole room into a walk-in wardrobe. That was pukka!

The bedroom has two main functions: rest and romance. To help me to rest, I like pastel colours on the walls – yellows, pinks, greys – and full-on, no-messing blackout blinds on the windows. One time, I made my own shutters out of floorboards! I'll explain how I did that later in this chapter on page 230.

Personally, I don't think romance should be limited to the bedroom – in a good, loving relationship, it can happen all around the house! So, I'm not into four-poster beds and all of that cheesy palaver, but I do love candles in the bedroom. They can set a really cool mood and vibe.

You'll have realized by now that I don't like my décor to be too busy, and that definitely goes for the bedroom. You don't want too much visual stimulation before you go to sleep, so I never have a television in the bedroom. It feels too eighties to me. I just don't need it.

TV may be banned in my boudoir but music certainly isn't! In one gaff, I put surround sound in the entire house by installing speakers under the floorboards, then drilling a group of small holes in the floor and ceiling above and below. Lie in bed and turn on surround-sound music via Bluetooth? Pure heaven!

We all have our own idea of heaven, and yours may not be the same as mine. How do you want to kit out your bedroom? Do you love bare floorboards or rugs? Blinds or luscious curtains? How about lighting? If you're working with a small bedroom, what are the best space-saving solutions?

Question, questions, questions about the most intimate room in your home, and the one that you spend more hours of your life in than any other. So, let's roll up our sleeves and find some right answers . . .

Clothes Storage

Nearly every bedroom has a wardrobe for hanging up clothes and some drawers for folded items and your smalls. Well, this is a perfectly decent system, but these are not the only way to store your clothes.

Some people find themselves 'storing' a lot of clothes in the ironing pile. That is definitely not the way to a calm and stress-free life! I like to have all my clothes clean, ironed and ready to wear. In fact, I sometimes wonder if I should have joined the Army. Sergeant Jay!

I prefer open storage so I can see my clothes choices as soon as I walk in the room, but I know that approach isn't for everyone. As with all of my advice in this book, the key to what you do is to figure out what will work best for you.

WARDROBES

Once, it was only wealthy people that had these, but today you'd be surprised to find any bedroom without a wardrobe. They provide easy hanging space and you can shut the door – or doors – to keep dust and damaging sunlight off the fabric of your clobber.

Do make sure you go through that rail at least once a year, though. Too often wardrobes are bulging with way too many clothes – half of which should have gone to the charity shop or been passed to the recycling centre, a long time ago. Share the love, and the old shirts!

I'm a real fan of old, solid furniture that was built to last by proper craftspeople. The dark-brown style might not be to everyone's taste, but here's the thing – you can always paint it!

I'm not a philistine. I'm not recommending painting precious antiques, but take it from me: there's plenty of good-quality furniture out there, in charity shops or online, just begging for a new home and to be given a new lease of life.

❯❯ Painting a wardrobe

Want to give your wardrobe a lick of paint? Before you start, make sure you give it a really good clean, especially in any nooks and crannies. Hot soapy water and a soft cloth with that trusty old toothbrush for those awkward spots should get the job done.

For the best results, lightly sand down the surfaces you want to paint, then wipe off any dust with a damp cloth. Once you've got a clean, dry, roughened surface, you're ready to rock 'n' roll.

The paint you use is up to you. Any paint that is suitable for woodwork will be great on a wooden wardrobe. (See page 130 for more on this.) Be careful with the doors – you'll probably need to prop them open while they dry.

>> Revamping a wardrobe

If you don't like the way your old wardrobe looks, don't just heave it out. There are all sorts of things you can do to breathe new life into it and have it looking tip-top again.

As I've already said, painting is one option, and it doesn't have to be limited to old darkwood furniture. So long as you can create the sort of surface that paint will stick to, you can give it a coat of colour that you really like.

In any case, don't limit yourself to paint. How about sticking patterned wallpaper to your furniture? It might sound a bit wacky, but I love doing this, and it means you can get a beautiful pattern onto your wardrobe without having to paint it on yourself.

For wardrobes with panelled doors, you could just paper the panels, or you could be more subtle and paper the sides of the wardrobe instead. Or how about the insides of the doors? Just imagine how chuffed that will make you feel every time you open them!

Another effective option is to change the handles. This simple step can really alter the overall look of a piece of furniture. And if you choose replacements that fit the same holes, you'll have a mini-revamp in no time at all.

Jay's Top Tip

Changing doors on wardrobes is another way to change the style, but take care when it comes to weight, and make sure your new doors aren't loads heavier than the originals.

CHESTS OF DRAWERS

Chests of drawers are the other staple of clothes storage. I can't stress this enough: quality really does matter here. How many times have you had the bottom fall out of a cheap and flimsy drawer? Even once is too many!

Again, there are plenty of second-hand, sturdy chests of drawers out there if you look. Do a tour of your local charity shops. These can often be revamped with new handles, refinishing or painting.

›› Fixing common drawer issues

There are other ways for drawers to malfunction besides their bottoms falling out. They can suffer from their runners getting misaligned, or, in older furniture, lose their 'glide'. For me, I can't abide lopsided drawers that won't shut properly, or a drawer that's so hard to pull out and push in that you feel like you've been to the gym every time you open it. No thank you!

PROBLEM	LIKELY CAUSE	SOLUTION
TOO HARD TO PULL OUT THE DRAWERS	This is common in older furniture that relies on wood sliding against wood. The problem is too much friction.	Reduce the friction. A bar of soap rubbed onto the parts that rub against each other should do the trick.
DRAWER IS ALIGNED BUT WON'T CLOSE	Something stuck down the back of the drawer? Something obstructing the rails or sliders towards the front of the drawer?	Get a torch and inspect all the drawers in the chest, comparing working drawers with the problem one. What's different? Figure that out and fix the issue.
BOTTOM KEEPS FALLING OUT OF THE DRAWER	The bottom has become bowed so it doesn't stay in its grooves.	Take the bottom out and cut a new one from the stiffest board you can find. It needs to be the same thickness as the original piece so it'll fit the grooves.
DRAWER IS LOPSIDED	One or both of the sliders/runners isn't working properly.	Take the drawer out completely and put it back carefully, aligning the runners. Does anything clunk? Is anything loose? Compare it to the other drawers and you might be able to diagnose and fix the issue.

CLOTHES STORAGE SYSTEMS

These are essentially giant wardrobes with drawers and shelves arranged inside them, as well as hanging rails. They're a popular bedroom option and can offer a fantastic storage solution to keep all your clothes and accessories in one place – but only if you keep them tidy. It's all too tempting to just chuck things in and shut the door.

If your storage system doesn't quite fit your needs, remember that even small tweaks can make a difference. Could you change the height of the shelves so you can insert some storage boxes? Would making the hanging rail a different height help?

This type of unit may have huge mirrored doors, which might not be your cup of tea. Think outside the box – could you spray them with frosting spray? Or stick on peelable window-obscuring film? It's got me wondering whether wallpaper would also stick to glass too . . . I'm gonna try that one.

HANGING RAILS

Give me a sturdy vintage hanging rail that's got a solid structure and a bit of wear to show it has an interesting life story, and I'm a happy man! Certainly far happier than I would be with a cheaply made version that wobbles like it's about to collapse.

A good hanging rail can be a great alternative to a wardrobe. However, be aware that your clothes can get a bit dusty as they are left uncovered. Also, if the rail stands in a spot that has strong sunlight at any part of the day, the colours of your clothing are likely to fade over time. I've seen these rails used really effectively in kids' bedrooms, though. They're ideal for their dressing-up clothes in particular.

CHESTS, TRUNKS AND CUPBOARDS

If you've got the space, a chest or bedding box at the foot of your bed is a great way to add flexible storage for folded out-of-season clothes, shoes, boots or bags. Even your spare bedding might fit in there.

We tend to associate wall-hung cupboards with kitchens more than any other room – but why? Here's a great home hack: you can use them really effectively to create your own version of a built-in bedroom.

STORAGE WALL

The real trick to this is to buy the widest wardrobes/floor-standing storage that will fit on each side of the bed.

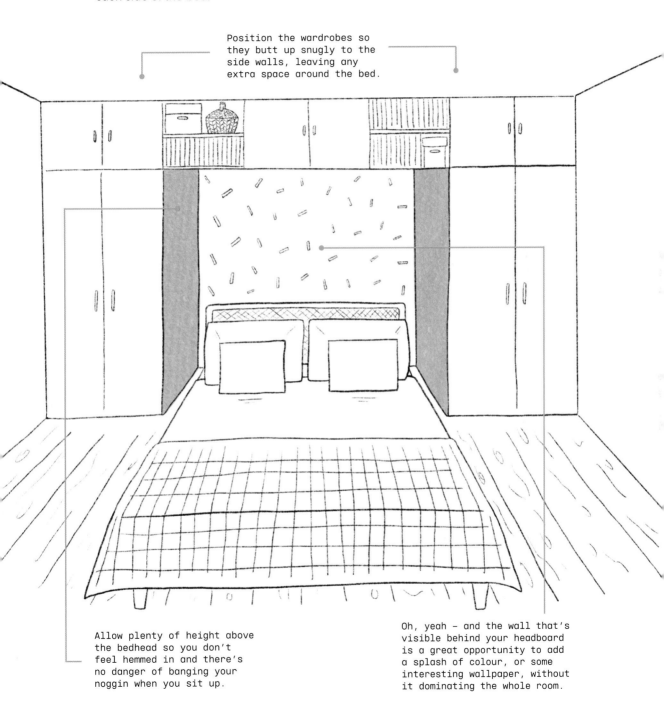

Position the wardrobes so they butt up snugly to the side walls, leaving any extra space around the bed.

Allow plenty of height above the bedhead so you don't feel hemmed in and there's no danger of banging your noggin when you sit up.

Oh, yeah – and the wall that's visible behind your headboard is a great opportunity to add a splash of colour, or some interesting wallpaper, without it dominating the whole room.

Built-in Storage

Building dedicated clothes storage into your bedroom can be a great way to maximize the space. And if you move somewhere with storage already built in that you don't like, or that doesn't fit your needs, you can get it altered by a carpenter or fix it yourself.

Switching the door handles, painting the doors or altering internal shelving are fairly straightforward jobs. However, if you want to swap hanging space for drawers or vice versa, make sure you don't remove any of the pieces that are needed to hold the whole thing together!

If you want to install built-in clothes storage, sure, there are umpteen companies who can do this for you. But here's the whole point of this book: why not do it yourself?

BUILDING INTO AN ALCOVE

If you've been blessed with a chimney breast in your bedroom, chances are you've got at least one alcove alongside it. It can be really tricky to make the most of that space, but it's absolutely perfect for a built-in wardrobe.

Jay's Top Tip

Here's a handy hint. If you can't face the idea of getting perfectly aligned doors, why not build the frame, with the hanging rail and the shelves above it inside, then install a roller blind or curtains across the front instead of doors?

You also need to bear in mind whether you want your storage to stick out beyond the depth of the alcove. Don't forget: if you're planning a hanging rail to go across the width, you'll need enough depth to the built-in wardrobe to accommodate your widest hangers. The standard wardrobe depth is 60cm.

As well as the basic work sequence shown here, you'll want to fill in any cracks, sand down all rough edges and possibly paint your masterpiece to match your walls.

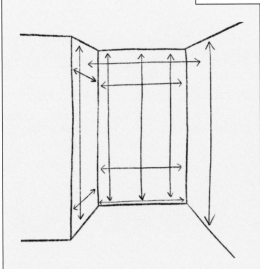

STEP 1

Measure the alcove's height, width and depth. Remember, the walls and ceiling may not be perfectly symmetrical and even, especially if you're in an older house, so take measurements at all the corners.

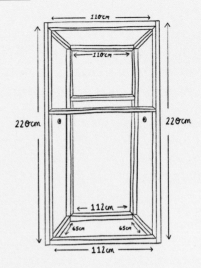

STEP 2

Sketch out a plan of the framework, including the position of the hanging rail and any shelves, and include the measurements so you can calculate the materials you need.

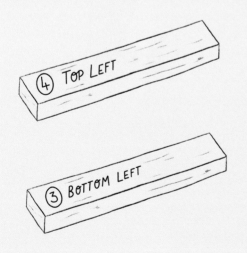

STEP 3

Cut the timber to length, label each part and attach the uprights to the wall.

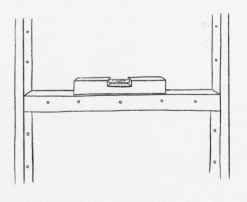

STEP 4

Attach the horizontals to the wall, ensuring the ones designed to take shelves are level. If you have a side panel to attach, do that next.

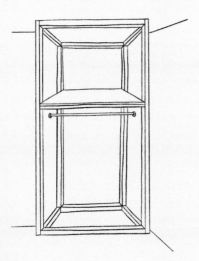

STEP 5

Check the measurements for any shelves and cut your timber to size. Insert the shelves and the hanging rail, attaching them to the horizontals or the sides of your frame/the walls.

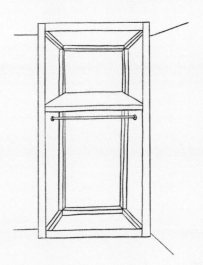

STEP 6

Whether you're adding doors or not, you'll need to add a fascia to the front of the frame for a neat, professional finish.

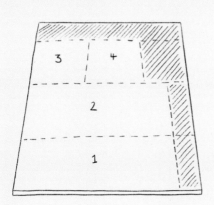

STEP 7

See page 67 for how to construct a simple door using battens and planks, or create your own from sheet timber. Check your original measurements and adjust if necessary, then cut or create the doors to fit.

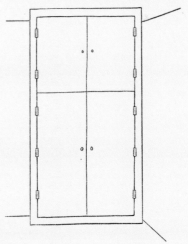

STEP 8

Hinges at the ready! Fit the largest doors first, then add magnetic closing mechanisms top and bottom, plus handles of your choice. Have you done all that? I take my cap off to you!

Carpet /

As I said at the start of the chapter, carpet is my number one choice of flooring for the bedroom – all day, every day. And the thicker and softer the better!

The carpet that really floats my boat is what we used to call shag pile back in the eighties but nowadays seems to have had a rebrand as 'deep pile'. (I suppose 'shag' was a bit of a funny word!) Basically, the tufts are nice and long so your feet sink into them. Lovely!

As far as I'm concerned, the same principle goes for rugs: the softer the better. But, obviously, I know that's not going to suit everybody. A deep-pile carpet or rug can be tricky to keep clean if you've got small children or pets, but if you can keep them out of your bedroom (good luck!) then you've got half a chance.

CARPET TYPES

There are so many carpet options that it can feel overwhelming. However, thinking about the pros and cons of each type can soon help you to narrow your options and make choosing the right one for your home and your family situation feel less intimidating.

›› Fibre type

Carpets are most commonly made from wool, polypropylene or polyamide (Nylon), but are also available in other natural materials such as sisal, cotton, seagrass and bamboo. There are pros and cons to each of these types, but wool is the best overall for most situations as it's natural, insulating, repels dirt and wears well.

›› Pile length

Generally speaking, the longer the pile, the thicker the carpet and the more I like it! It's also often more expensive and harder to keep in top condition, so although it pains me to tell you this, thicker doesn't always mean better.

» Pile type

This is much easier to understand with some pictures:

TWIST:
This type of cut pile gives a smooth and durable carpet that's easy to maintain.

SAXONY:
This cut pile is much denser, giving a more luxurious feel underfoot.

LOOP:
This has a different texture to cut-pile carpet but is more practical for high-traffic areas.

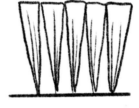

VELVET:
The smoothest of the cut-pile options, but not as hard-wearing as its cousins.

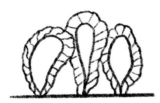

BERBER:
A dense type of loop pile that's very hard-wearing.

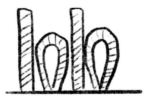

CUT AND LOOP:
This is a mix of the two pile types, where the loop pile gives a textural pattern to the cut pile.

UNDERLAY, UNDERLAY!

If you want your carpet to wear well, it's crucial to choose the highest-quality underlay you can afford. It acts as a cushion between your sub-floor and the carpet, which means that the carpet itself has physical support for all of the walking, crawling and playing that it will have to endure over its lifetime. There are four main types of underlay, each with slightly different properties:

- ### CRUMB RUBBER
  This is super-hardwearing and many manufacturers make it partly from old car tyres, (obviously, recycling is always cool). It's especially good for high-traffic areas, so maybe it's not the number one choice for your bedroom. The best thing about it is that it will last and last.

- ### FELT/CRUMB RUBBER COMBINATION
  This combination underlay is hardwearing and soft and is particularly good for insulating against sound and heat loss.

- ### SPONGE RUBBER
  This is the absolute classic style of underlay, even though nowadays it's more likely to be made from synthetic materials rather than natural rubber. It's springy to the touch and gives a great feel to the carpet, especially the thicker versions.

- ### POLYURETHANE
  This is becoming really popular, and with good reason. It's available in different grades and thicknesses to suit your subfloor-and-carpet combo and usually contains recycled foam: more good news for the planet!

FITTING CARPET

To be honest with you, in most circumstances I'd say this is a job best left to the professionals. Carpet and underlay need to be laid perfectly if they are going to last well and look good.

However, if you're carpeting a fairly simple-shaped room and you don't need to have joins in your carpet, then it's definitely do-able, as long as you have the right tools. You'll need a proper carpet stretcher and tucker as well as a dolphin-handled knife. The method of measuring the space is the same as for laying sheet vinyl – see pages 174–175. Oh, and remember to always transport your carpet rolled up. Never fold it!

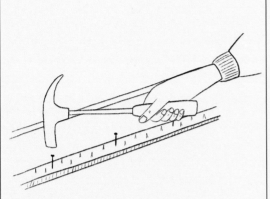

STEP 1

Ensuring your subfloor is clean and level (see page 60), fit carpet gripper strips around the sides of the room, tacking them down to secure them to the floor, but skipping the space in the doorway.

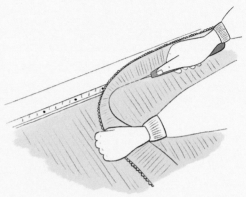

STEP 2

Next up is underlay. It needs to be fitted to butt up to but not be on top of the carpet grippers, and any joins should be taped together to give an even, level surface.

STEP 3

Lay the carpet in the room, loosely positioning it first so that you're 100 per cent certain it's the correct way around. Starting in one corner with one foot under the carpet, push and smooth it into place with the other foot. You want around 5–7cm extra all around the edge, so trim any excess over this once you're happy it is in the right position.

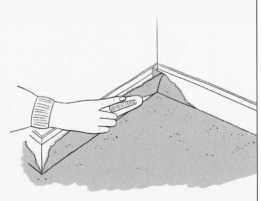

STEP 4

In each corner, cut a vertical line in the excess so the carpet can lie flat and trim off the overlapping triangles.

Step *by* Step

STEP 5

Now, you can start to fit your carpet! Bear in mind that it needs to be pulled taut across the room. Begin on the longest wall, and pick the corner furthest from the door. Firmly crease the carpet against the skirting board using a carpet tucker.

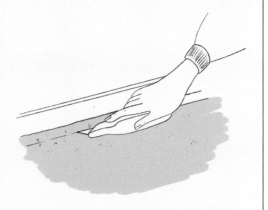

STEP 6

Cut the edge of the carpet about 5mm above the surface with a dolphin-handled knife (a utility knife with a shaped handle for better grip), holding the carpet flat to the floor as you go.

STEP 7

Position the teeth of the carpet stretcher about 2.5cm from the skirting board. Push the padded area firmly with your knee to stretch the carpet towards the skirting board. Push the edge down onto the gripper and tuck the excess under the skirting board with the tucker.

STEP 8

Continue in this way right along the wall, then work on the two adjacent walls, and finally the opposite wall. At the door threshold, trim the carpet to be flush with the flooring outside the room, and install a threshold strip to hide the join.

Cleaning Carpets

It's really important that you vacuum your carpet every week. And I mean all of it – not just the bits that look dirty!

Even the areas that don't get walked on much will have gathered dust, and the best way to keep your carpet looking good for years and years is to keep it clean. Yet vacuuming is the easy part – what about dealing with those inevitable spills, splats and other accidents?

- Blot away or scrape off as much of the mess as possible with a clean cloth or piece of kitchen towel.

- DON'T scrub or rub the carpet. You may get rid of the stain, but scrubbing will destroy the pile and leave you with a worn patch.

- With a cloth and a bowl of hot water, gently blot more of the stain away. Work from the outer edges of the mark towards the middle.

- Blot again with a clean, dry cloth. If you have some carpet cleaner, test it on an inconspicuous part of the carpet.

- Weak white-vinegar solution is a good all-round carpet cleaner that's safe on all fibres. Simply put a tablespoon of white vinegar in a small bowl and top up with warm water. Mix, then use this to blot the stain with a cloth.

- If your carpet still needs help, it's time to either use the cleaner you've just tested or buy a stain remover. If you do the latter, be sure to check it's appropriate for your type of stain, and safe for your type of carpet.

 Jay's Top Tip

Always keep some of the offcuts of your carpet – you can test cleaning products on them or, worst case scenario, use them to patch into irretrievably damaged carpet.

Rugs

I believe The Verve once said that 'The Rugs Don't Work' (or something like that: I couldn't hear the radio very clearly). Well, they were wrong! Rugs are a great way to add texture, colour and cosiness to your bedroom – and the rest of your home – without breaking the bank, and you can take them with you whenever you move house!

Rugs are often made from the same materials as carpet, so the same rules apply when it comes to care and cleaning. But new innovations are being made all the time, especially with regard to sustainability. Did you know you can get really soft-feeling rugs made from recycled plastic bottles? Well, you do now!

In a bedroom, I love to have something super-soft and fluffy to put my feet onto when I get out of bed. But everyone's priorities are different. Just make sure that you choose a style, colour and texture that add a bit of wow to your room.

SIZE AND SCALE

When you're choosing a rug, or rugs, be careful about getting the size right in relation to the room. It's all very well going for the fluffiest, most luxurious-looking rug, but if it's too small for the room it's going to look silly, like a tiny island floating in an ocean of floor. And if it's too big, you risk it taking over.

A good way to think about placing rugs is to 'anchor' them next to or even underneath a piece of furniture, or place parallel to a wall. Leave a gap of up to about 30cm and it should look like a good fit.

Jay's Top Tip

If you're putting your rug on a hard floor, it could be a slip hazard. In that case, it's important to get an anti-slip mat of some sort to fit underneath it so it stays in place and you don't come a cropper.

Curtains & Blinds

Sleep, glorious sleep! We all love it, and it's so much easier to get some decent shut-eye if your windows don't let in street noise, draughts or the morning sun. As well as being a practical addition to any bedroom, curtains act as a frame for your window when they're open, and offer a great opportunity to add colour and texture to your room.

There are lots of different systems for hanging curtains. However, the principle is always the same: you need some sort of hooks, at regular intervals, at the top of the curtains to attach to a pole or track, allowing the curtains to be opened and closed easily. The heavier the curtains, the more robust the pole needs to be.

CURTAIN POLES

Your window may already have a curtain pole in place, and you may not need to replace it, as long as it's compatible with your curtains and your room design.

Curtain poles usually have some sort of decorative ends. These can be changed if you don't like them, or the style no longer suits your room. You can also paint wooden curtain poles: treat them as you would any wood. (See page 93 for more on painting wood.)

Poles are always partly visible, especially if you're combining them with eyelet curtains (more on these on page 217). So, if the style and feel of the pole really clashes with your new look, changing it is the best option.

CURTAIN TRACK

Where curtain poles are always partly visible, curtain track is designed to be as inconspicuous as possible. There are different types but they tend to be pretty similar in form. Track is flexible so it's ideal for awkward room shapes such as curved bay windows. It can be cut to length pretty easily, too, with a small hacksaw.

>> Getting good glide

Track that's been in place for a while can become hard to use because the sliding loops can get sticky. Thankfully, you can sort out this particular problem very quickly.

If you've had any building work done, or even if you live on a busy road, there's a good chance that fine gritty particles have got lodged in your curtain track. The best fix for this is to take out the little sliding loops (try twisting them up at 45 degrees and they'll usually pop out) and clean them in hot, soapy water.

Get a cloth and dip it in the water. Wipe the track to get it clean, pushing the cloth into the groove at the back. Once everything is clean and dry, spray some furniture polish on the back of the track, into the groove, and buff it up with a cloth.

THE CURTAINS

You don't need me to tell you how many options there are when it comes to curtains. What's really important is to get the right fit, and that means width as well as length.

Some curtains are designed with pleats at the top. This give a really opulent feel, not least because they are often made with thick, luxury fabrics such as velvet or brocade. Others have big eyelets so that they fit directly onto the pole, with no need for hooks.

If you have (or are making) curtains that are gathered using curtain tape at the top, remember that it can be tightened and loosened to fit your windows perfectly. Also, most tape has several options for where to put the little hooks, meaning you can vary the horizontal positioning of the curtains on your track.

>> The right fit

Curtains should either come down to the floor and just touch it, or finish slightly below the windowsill. Think of them as like trousers; long trousers are OK, shorts are fine, but nothing in between, thank you very much!

The positioning of the pole or track is crucial. You need to place it around 10cm above the top of the window. It also needs to extend well beyond the sides of the window – enough to accommodate all of the fabric when the curtains are open – so that all the light from the window can flood into the room unhindered.

EYELETS, HOOKS OR PINS?

How you attach your curtains to your pole or track is often decided by what is going on at the top of the curtains. But there is an element of choice, and your fixings can have an effect on the way the curtains hang.

If you are buying your curtains from a shop, ask the assistant for advice on hanging them and which hooks they would recommend.

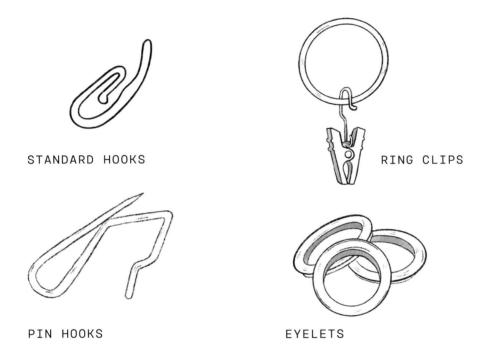

STANDARD HOOKS

RING CLIPS

PIN HOOKS

EYELETS

CURTAIN ALTERATIONS

If you're taking up curtains, leave as much fabric in the hem as you can. This gives flexibility if you want to transfer them to your next bedroom (or any other room) and the added weight also will help your curtains to hang properly. It's a win-win!

If your curtains are too short, you've got a couple of options. If there's enough fabric, let down the hem, then iron gently on the reverse of the fabric to remove the crease of the old hem before re-hemming to the correct length.

If that still isn't enough, you might be able to alter the top fixings to let the curtains hang lower. For example, you could use ring clips instead of hooks. As a last resort, you can lower your curtain track or pole.

FINISHING TOUCHES

If your curtains are especially thick, you'll need to help them tuck back from your window with holdbacks or tiebacks. If you think laterally here, it's a good chance to get creative and add some interesting detail.

A holdback is simply a big hook attached to the wall at the side of the window recess. It needs to be big enough for all the gathered fabric to fit into without causing creases. They are usually made of metal, and the range is staggering.

If you already have holdbacks but don't like the style, perhaps you could revamp them? Something as simple as taking them off the wall and outside for a quick coat of spray paint can leave them looking spectacular.

Tiebacks are rope loops that you loop around the curtain to 'tie' it back (hence the name!) and that are then fixed to smaller hooks attached to the wall. Traditionally these have beautiful tassels, but you could really go to town with beads, pompoms or anything else that goes with the design of your room.

Blinds

From roller to Roman, there's a blind for every type of window and style of décor. Perhaps you don't want the busyness and bulkiness of thick curtains in your bedroom? In that case, a blind is a great option. If you're a light sleeper or a night-shift worker, you could install blackout blinds to keep out daylight while you sleep. This will also enable you to use more lightweight curtains in the window because they won't need to block out light, draughts and noise. Blackout blinds are also great for helping to create a nighttime environment to get babies to sleep during the day!

PERFECT FIT

We've said that curtains should always extend above and to each side of the window recess. By contrast, blinds can be inserted right into the recess, which gives a more streamlined look to your room and increases the sense of spaciousness.

Roller blinds are often customizable, so you can cut them down to fit the width of a recess perfectly. Venetian and Roman blinds come in a good range of widths so, while you can't customize them, you should be able to find one that will work for your window, and some home furnishing stores will offer made-to-measure services if you can't.

BLACKOUT BLINDS

Blackout blinds are made from fabric that blocks out absolutely all of the light. However, you'll only achieve a proper blackout effect if the blind fits the window recess perfectly, slotting into tracks at the side of the window reveal, or if you install it on the wall above the window with plenty of blind extending above, below and to both sides.

BLINDS FOR ROOF WINDOWS

If any of your rooms are in the loft or attic, chances are you've got some sloping windows set into the roof. Unless you work for NASA and have a home anti-gravity chamber, curtains are not an option there!

Blinds are the best option for these roof windows, but it's vital that you buy ones that are made to fit – they usually sit behind a frame to hold them against the glass. They are easy to fit yourself, although if you need ladders to reach them you'll need to have another person to hand things up to you. You're not an octopus, mate!

Shutters

I'm a big fan of shutters and, I must admit, I'm quite proud of some of the ones I've made over the years. In some ways, shutters are the most primitive kind of window cover, but they don't have to look rough and ready. They work particularly well if you have a deep windowsill or a bay window because you can make them to fit perfectly.

SHUTTER STYLES

Window shutters generally come in three styles:

1 **PLANTATION STYLE**: With moveable wooden slats so you can control the light coming into your room from the windows.

2 **LOUVERED**: Where smaller slats are fixed at an angle so some light always comes through.

3 **SOLID**: Shaker-style ones have panelling rather than a flat wooden surface, and board and batten ones are constructed from vertical board held in place with battens on the back. This kind are the simplest to construct yourself.

For elsewhere in the house, you may consider café-style shutters, which only cover the bottom half of the window. However, I'm assuming that all of us require a little bit more privacy in our boudoirs!

There are plenty of companies out there that will make shutters to fit your windows. They're a great option if you're lucky enough to have the budget, as they aren't cheap! But I've always made my own – like everything, it's easy when you know how.

MAKING YOUR OWN SHUTTERS

I'm going to show you how to make concertina shutters using simple planks that fold back into the window reveal. Bear in mind that for a bay window, you can use the same principle and have fewer, wider panels that fold back against the internal wall.

You may read this and think, Jay! Using multiple hinges for each join is a right faff! But, trust me, it will make your shutters more robust, and your visitors will be admiring them for years to come.

Step *by* Step

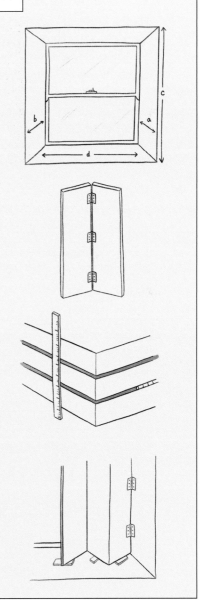

STEP 1

Measure your planks and window carefully, including the width of the window frames and the depth of the recess. Calculate how many planks you'll need to cover the window area, with about 1cm to spare all the way around the edge.

STEP 2

Once you've got your planks and cut them to length, join them together with hinges so that they fold up like a concertina.

STEP 3

Be careful about keeping the planks level as you keep adding more, and check the edges are level after each addition.

STEP 4

Half-unfold each concertina and prop it with offcuts so it is sitting 1cm above the sill. Then mark and attach hinges between the shutter and the window frame.

Internal Doors

Isn't it always a great feeling to close your bedroom door at the end of every day, ready for a good night's kip? Yeah, but only if your door shuts properly and you like the way it looks! Happily, there are plenty of things you can do to fix common door issues and change the way they look without breaking either the bank or your back. So, bring it on!

REVAMPING OLD DOORS

If your internal doors look dated, or you don't like the colour, a lick of paint might be all you need. Remember that you can always paint the inside of the door a different colour to the outside. If you're feeling adventurous, why not paint the edge of the door in a contrast colour?

If you've got those flat, plain, deep-brown wooden doors so popular in the seventies and eighties, you could take advantage of the flatness of the surface and wallpaper it! Why not? Just remember to remove the handle carefully first, then use a utility knife to trim around the hole where it needs to fit back on.

REPLACING DOORS

A word to the wise when it comes to replacing doors: you need to be careful with regard to building regulations. If they're fire doors, you'll need to replace them with other fire doors, and these require specialist fitting.

If they're not fire doors, you're good to go. Ensure your measurements are accurate, and be prepared to saw or plane a little bit off the bottom or sides to get a perfect fit. Be realistic. It's a challenging but do-able job, but if you don't have the right tools, it may be worth getting a carpenter in to do it for you. This is one of those crucial home-fix jobs where experience counts for a lot.

FIXING COMMON DOOR ISSUES

You won't need a chippy for these. You can solve nearly all common door problems yourself. These include doors that stick, won't stay shut, let in light or draughts or have an annoying tendency to slam.

>> Latch problems

If your door won't stay shut or is difficult to open, take a good look at the latch. Does it line up properly with the hole in the strike plate on the frame? Give the handle or knob a twist: does the latch fully retract and extend? You could try oiling it and see if that helps, but replacing a latch isn't expensive and is probably the best long-term solution.

>> Handle or doorknob problems

Do you twist the handle and the latch doesn't move immediately? This is because sometimes the internal mechanism where the handle shaft is attached to the latch end can work loose.

So, carefully take the latch and handle apart and see what's going on. Something loose? Try tightening it! As with dismantling a bathroom tap (see page 181), work methodically so you can retrace your steps to put it back together again.

>> Draught and light problems

These can usually be fixed by adding a draughtproofing brush seal strip to the bottom of the door. These come in various lengths, so measure the gap that's letting the light and draught through and take it from there.

>> Slamming problems

Internal doors often have a mechanism to ensure they stay closed, but sometimes the action is a bit too vigorous. It can lead to you slamming doors behind you even when you haven't got the raving hump! Here's what you do to sort this out. First off, check the hinges. If any of the screws have worked loose, it can unbalance the door. Tighten any loose screws and see if that does the trick.

If it doesn't, try felt pads. These are usually used on the bottom of wooden furniture legs. However, if you position small ones at the top and bottom of the frame, on the surface that the door slams into, they can really make a difference to the level of noise.

Beds

The most important element of any bedroom. My advice is simple here: make sure that yours is comfortable for you and you love the way it looks. If you take one look at your bed and you can't wait to dive into it, happy days!

If your bed – or mattress – has seen better days, don't put off getting an upgrade. Good sleep is the foundation of good health, so don't underestimate the power of a comfy bed on your overall well-being.

BEDFRAMES

Over the years, I have made so many bed frames out of old pallets! They are perfect for the job. They offer a sturdy, level platform and they allow air to circulate all around your mattress.

Not for you? Fair enough, but ensure that whatever kind of bed frame you go for lifts your mattress off the floor, offers a really stable base for it, and is the right height for you to sink into or climb out of. If your bedframe is wobbly or creaky, tighten all the screws – they do come loose over time.

WHAT SIZE IS BEST?

If you ask me, the bigger the better! But not everyone feels that way, especially if they aren't in danger of their feet dangling off the end like I am with my big, gangly frame.

If you're lucky enough to have a sizeable bedroom, it's definitely a good idea to go for a really big bed so that proportionally it looks good. But remember, the bigger the bed, the bigger the duvet, and the more challenging it can be to change the bedding! Especially on your tod!

Jay's Top Tip

It's super important that your bed frame and mattress are the same size. This may sound impossible to get wrong, but, trust me, people do! Watch the length, especially with double beds.

SIZE	WIDTH	LENGTH
SMALL SINGLE	75CM	190CM
SINGLE	90CM	190CM
EUROPEAN SINGLE	90CM	200CM
SMALL DOUBLE/QUEEN	120CM	190CM
DOUBLE	135CM	190CM
EUROPEAN DOUBLE	140CM	200CM
KINGSIZE	150CM	200CM
EUROPEAN KINGSIZE	160CM	200CM
SUPERKING	180CM	200CM

BUNK BEDS

Bagsy me on top! Bunk beds are every kid's dream bed, but there are a few pitfalls to bear in mind.

Changing the sheet on the top bunk can be a challenge, depending on its height (and yours!). Although top bunks are always designed with a side rail for safety, make sure whoever sleeps up there is steady on the ladders.

And a handy medical hint: if you've got a kid with a poorly tummy, put them in the bottom bunk, with easier access to the bathroom. Those precious few seconds can make all the difference!

MATTRESSES

My advice here could not be simpler: choose a mattress that you love the feel of. Don't muck about or settle for second-best: pick a high-quality one that will last for years, and give you hours and hours of restorative shut-eye every night.

It's always advisable to try before you buy. If you have a partner, test mattresses together (don't worry, furniture-shop assistants are used to it!).

Does one of you love firm mattresses while the other prefers them soft? Well, believe it or not, you can get mattresses that are hard on one side and soft on the other. This means there is something suitable for every couple, no matter how picky they are when it comes to getting those precious zzzzzs.

- **OPEN SPRING:** A network of metal springs covered by thick padding. These mattresses tend to be budget-friendly but can have a tendency to sink in the middle over time.

- **POCKET SPRING:** The metal springs in these mattresses are in separate pockets and therefore tend to be better at responding to individual movement.

- **MEMORY FOAM:** These mould themselves to your body and are usually loved by side-sleepers. They're not for everyone though so try before you buy!

- **BED-IN-A-BOX:** This is a hybrid of memory foam and other types of foam and/or springs and comes rolled in a box. A useful tip: they often have a long returns policy that allows you to try it at home for a number of weeks to see if you like it.

My Favourite...

HEADBOARD

There's something about the way I see the world that definitely shapes how I approach home décor. I don't know whether this a visual tic that is linked to my dyslexia, but I often see an object and imagine it being used in a way that is not its intended purpose.

Do you know what I mean? No? Well, let me explain . . .

Walking down the street one day, I saw two mahogany wardrobe doors leaning against a garden wall, with a sign saying 'TAKE ME'. I did, like a shot! They were from a 1920s wardrobe, with lovely carvings around the outside, and I thought they could make a great table.

Craftsmen made things proper in the old days, from solid timber, and I had a job on to cart the doors back home. But once I had done it, I had a second thought: Hang on a minute! Never mind a table – what about using these as a bedhead and footboard?

So, that was what I did. I lugged the doors into the bedroom and set one at the head of the bed. I didn't need to put it on stilts and attach it to the bed, like headboards normally are: I just secured it directly to the wall and slid the bed under it.

It looked fantastic, especially when I fastened the second door to the other end of the bed to use as the footboard. I didn't need to paint or varnish either of them: the mahogany already had a nice rich colour, so they looked perfect just as they were.

I accessorised our new bed by re-upholstering a couple of chairs in colours that looked great with them, and – voilà! A cool and co-ordinated bedroom at almost no cost at all! There's a lot to be said for lateral thinking.

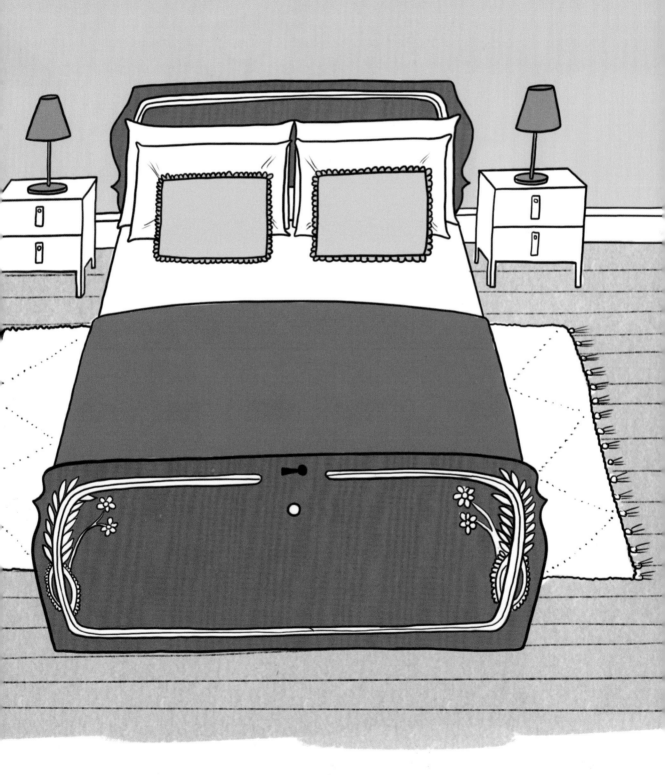

Outdoor

Spaces

Gardens and outdoor spaces should be a big part of your daily life, especially in warmer months of summer.

They say it's better to be beautiful on the inside than the outside and, on the whole, I agree with that. But why not do both? So when you're on a revamping and DIY binge and turning your gaff into a palace, make sure you don't neglect those all-important outdoor areas.

Don't think of them as separate entities. Gardens and outdoor spaces should be a big part of your daily life, especially in the warmer months of summer. I love nothing more than having a barbecue for mates on a balmy August evening – but I will only enjoy it if the place is looking proper.

I'll confess straight up that I'm not a gardener. It's not something that I'm into. That means when it comes to planning outdoor spaces, I'm looking for something that will look good and be fun to chill out in and demands only the minimum amount of input and work from me.

Your front garden, if you are lucky enough to have one, is important because it is the first thing your guests will see. Front spaces tend to be quite small, so why not do something like a Japanese garden, with slates and stones, rather than a postage-stamp bit of grass? They look great and are a cinch to maintain.

Chances are that most of the action will happen in your back garden. That's where you're more likely to hang out in good weather, and there are loads of great décor and DIY tips to make sure that your long summer evenings out there are well enjoyable.

My ideal garden has a lawn (I love mowing it to get those Wimbledon stripes!) and a decking area to socialize on, plus a nice rockery. I also love an outdoor office that might be a little bit open-plan, so you can set your music up in there and blast it out when you are partying.

Lighting is important to set the mood in a garden, and I'm a fan of the big white globe balls you can find in any DIY or garden centre. You can have a timer to come on at dusk or even get solar-powered ones, and they really help to set up a cool mood in the evenings.

When it comes to laying decking, a lot of people sensibly get in the professionals, but if you're up for some really hard graft it's definitely a job you can take on yourself! I've never been prouder of a DIY job than I was when I built my own decking-board seating. I'll tell you all about that on pages 264–265.

You can sit on anything in the garden – benches, garden chairs or deck chairs, beanbags, whatever floats your boat!

You need a bit of privacy in your garden and, for me, it's fences over hedges all day, every day. Hedges are too much hard work! I've built big fences around houses I've lived in before, using fence posts and boards. I'll tell you how to fix them securely so the wind can't blow them over.

You can sit on anything in the garden – benches, garden chairs or deck chairs, beanbags, whatever floats your boat! I like to create a seating area on the decking, with a dining table and wooden seats that lift up to reveal storage areas within. That neatly solves two problems in one.

When you've got your garden in shape, you'll want to have a few gatherings of friends and family to show it off. I love barbecues – it's about the only cooking I do! You can just buy them, of course, but I once built my own one out of an old oil drum. I loved flipping burgers and having a good chinwag over that!

As a non-gardener, for me, a shed isn't essential – I can keep the few tools I have in those handy decking seats (I even managed to squeeze in my lawnmower!) – but a work office is. I know, with the Covid pandemic, so many of us were working from home, but I'm not a fan of my house being cluttered with keyboards, monitors and laptops. Years ago, when I was first working from home regularly I levelled an area of garden, laid some foundations, bought a garden office that came in big panels that simply needed fixing together . . . and, voila! The world's easiest commute!

If you live in a town or city, your garden is the closest you get to nature on a daily basis, so it's nice to let it all flourish. I'd much rather plant a tree than stick in a gazebo or some such. It's better for your wellbeing and the environment. And why not extend a helping hand to wildlife? I like my garden to have a few bug hotels, which you can easily build from recycled materials like leftover bricks and/or broken bamboo garden canes. Bugs and insects will live there through the winter, protected from the elements. Hedgehog hotels are similar, but bigger and more structured. I draw the line at foxes, mind. They're just pests!

So, how do you turn your outside spaces into gardens of delight? What are the secrets of decking and landscaping, what kind of garden path will work the best, and – most important of all – is there any place in this day and age for garden gnomes? Pick up your spade and follow me . . .

Kerb Appeal

Do you know what kerb appeal is? Well, if you watched any of the major property shows that were all over the telly in the noughties, it is a phrase you'll definitely be familiar with!

Basically, it's dead important to make sure that walking up to your own front door is as pleasant an experience as possible. And I don't mean just to impress your friends and family, I'm talking about your own sense of wellbeing here.

Approaching your gaff every day is when you get your first impression of your home, your safe haven, and although it might not register in your conscious mind, that moment can have such a beneficial effect on you psychologically. So, think about these questions:

Do you like your front door? Are you happy with the general tidiness and overall look of the front of your house? Be honest: does anything need repairing or repainting? Well, if so, don't put it off!

THE FRONT DOOR

I've already talked about the front door on page 146. It has to be secure and keep you warm and safe indoors (and the cold safely outside). But you also need to think about the door's aesthetics – and make sure that it looks and feels tip-top.

My favourite type of front door is a wooden one. Yeah, yeah, you need to repaint them from time to time, and they can warp a little bit over the years, but for me, a solid chunk of timber between my home and the outside world is absolutely the way to go. The advantage is that you can fairly easily change the colour and finish by repainting it – which gives it an instant new look.

But front doors aren't only about the colour. There's the door furniture to think of, which is a fancy way of saying anything that attaches to the door – such as your house number, knocker, letterbox, or anything else that's stuck on it. Most people hardly give those things a thought, but you'll be surprised just how different your door can look if you change them!

FRONT OF HOUSE

Here's a little exercise for you. Go and stand outside your house and take a good butcher's at it. Look up and down your street, too, and see what your neighbours' houses look like. Are there some that look nicer than others to you?

Now, get your thinking cap on. What can you do to raise your front-of-house game?

Just off the top of my noggin, here are a few suggestions:

- Clean not just your windows but also the windowsills and window surrounds.
- Spruce up the garden or any plant pots you've got outside.
- Sweep up dead leaves, litter and general street grime.

What can you add to make your home look more welcoming? Plants are great, but bear in mind you'll need to water them! Could you improve on any bin storage you have? Is your hedge/fence/wall/gate in need of some serious TLC?

It may seem an intimidating task, but it's not: it'll take far less time and effort than you imagine to have your front space looking blinding. So, don't hold back and don't delay!

SEE IN THE DARK

We've got more general info about outdoor lighting on page 257, but here's a basic yet important tip for you: at the front of your house, make sure there is enough light to see the door and so you can find your keys when you get home in the dark. Because who wants to be swearing and fiddling with a bunch of keys every evening?

Personally, I love playing with lighting through plant foliage to create beautiful silhouettes. If you've got the space, it can make a front garden look fantastic. But on a more practical level, a simple security light that operates on a sensor, which will come on when there is movement outside your front door, is practical, helpful and good for peace of mind security-wise.

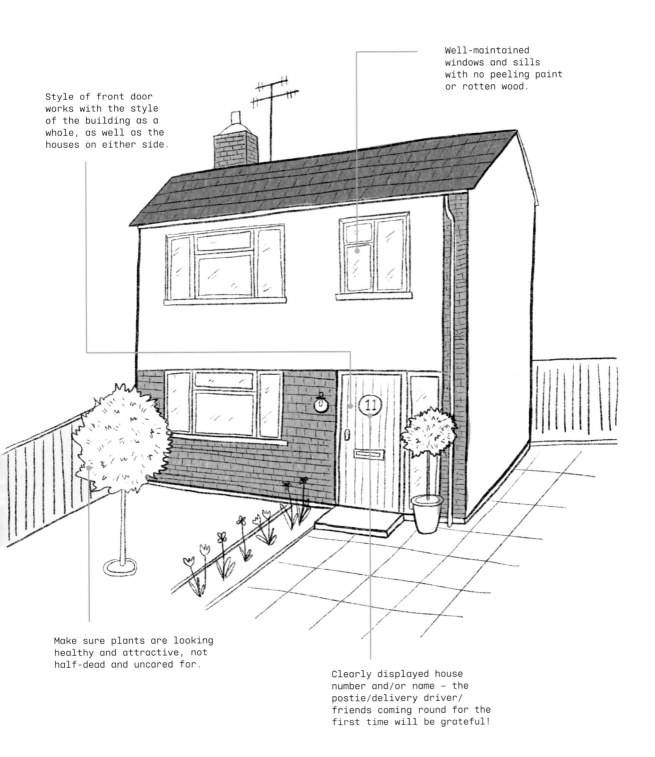

Style of front door
works with the style
of the building as a
whole, as well as the
houses on either side.

Well-maintained
windows and sills
with no peeling paint
or rotten wood.

Make sure plants are looking
healthy and attractive, not
half-dead and uncared for.

Clearly displayed house
number and/or name – the
postie/delivery driver/
friends coming round for the
first time will be grateful!

Garden Seating

For some folks, a garden is all about herbaceous borders. For others, it's having it as a veg plot that floats their boat. For me, it's about having a space where I feel at peace, with comfy seating to chill in, whether I'm socializing with family and friends, or all on my Jack Jones.

If you're lucky enough to have a sturdy tree or two in your garden, stretching a hammock between them is an easy way to get some serious relaxing done. I can even pretend I'm back in the Caribbean, when the British weather lets me! (Which I admit isn't very often . . .)

FLEXIBILITY

Socializing outside is usually nice and laid back. If your outside space is any bigger than the size of a picnic rug, you've got a few options when it comes to sitting out there.

Nostalgia time: do you remember when you were a kid and sitting on the floor was totally comfy? Well, I don't feel that way any more, not now I've reached the ripe old age of lower-back twinges, and I think most adults over thirty will agree. We need a bit of lumbar support!

I reckon the best approach to garden seating is to have a mix of options to suit different needs. Have seats you can move close to each other if you've got friends or family round and you want a good natter. Make sure there's somewhere that's perfect for relaxing in the sun with a good book and a cold beverage.

We all do more than one thing in the garden, so, whatever style you go for, just make sure it is flexible and can cater for all of your outdoor social needs.

DECKCHAIRS AND FOLDING CHAIRS

Sometimes, the old ways are the best. Proper old-school deckchairs are brilliant! They are really comfy, and they fold away so you don't need too much space to store them.

Despite that, there are plenty of more modern equivalents. Have a gander in a DIY store catalogue at camping chairs. They often have a drinks holder in the chair arm. Bosh – what more can you ask for?

Chairs that fold up for storage are perfect for small spaces. It means you can put out just the right number each time, and not clutter up your outdoor space with chairs that aren't being sat on – and they're easy to put away in winter.

SWING SEATS AND HAMMOCKS

There is something about swinging or swaying gently in the fresh air that instantly puts us in a holiday mood (especially if you spend time visiting your mum in Barbados, like I do!). It's really tempting to go for this type of seating at home, but make sure you've got enough room. Sadly, your back space ain't a beach!

Hammocks take up a surprisingly large amount of space, especially if you need a frame for them. And I have to confess that, much as I love them, they're a bit of a selfish pleasure and not ideal for socializing.

Swing seats come in a massive range of types and sizes and usually have 'all-weather' cushions to make them comfy. Now, 'all-weather' is a bit of a misleading phrase. Just because the cushions can withstand some sun, rain, hail and snow doesn't mean they'll still look nice come the end of winter! So find somewhere dry you can store them over the colder months to stop them getting mouldy.

OUTDOOR SOFAS

These have been fashionable for a while now, and I can see why – the comfort of a sofa in your garden? Yes, please! As with swing seats, though, remember that the cushions will need storing somewhere dry over the winter and whenever it rains in summer (let's face it, it happens!). If you leave them outside permanently, they get discoloured and well manky around the edges.

Shop around for the best configuration for your space. Some ranges are 'modular', meaning that each seat can be separated from its neighbour, leaving you free to arrange them how you want, depending on who's coming over.

BEANBAGS AND THEIR INFLATABLE FRIENDS

I love outdoor beanbags – they bring out everyone's inner child! If you can see a beanbag lying in a garden and not have a crafty bounce onto it, you're a better man than me! Or, at least, a more grown-up one . . .

The main difference between outdoor and indoor beanbags is the fabric they are covered with. Outdoor ones have tough, synthetic fibres because they are resistant to mould and mildew (and may even survive if a passing cat or fox fancies a chew on them!). Again, though, I would advise bringing them indoors for the winter and on rainy days.

Confession time: the outdoor chairs that I really want a go on, but haven't done yet, are the ones you inflate just by running down your garden with them. No, I'm not on drugs! These chairs are basically giant plastic bags covered in lightweight fabric with a smart roll-top fastening that holds the air in. They look well comfy! Once you're done, you simply let the air out, roll the chair up and marvel at how little space it takes up!

Now that is definitely one for my next birthday wish list . . .

Jay's Top Tip

Built-in seating is a great addition to any garden (see pages 264–265) but especially in small spaces, and even better if it can double up as storage. It doesn't have to do this of course – although, for me, any seat with a space underneath it needs hinges added to make use of it, otherwise, it's just wasted space. And I hate that.

Outdoor Cooking

There's something so primal about cooking over flames outdoors. It's been a while since one of my rare days off was sunny enough for me to have a barbecue, but you can't beat socializing and chowing down right there in your own garden.

It's the business! Ah, the smell of grilling sausages! Chargrilled corn on the cob! Tasty kebabs! It all turns me into a right happy urban caveman.

I love a good old-fashioned barbecue but there are tons of other options for cooking outdoors. Pizza ovens are a really popular choice. You can get the temperature in them much higher than you can in a domestic oven, so your pizza will be that much more crispy and delicious.

Oh, and if you want a well luxurious option, there are egg-shaped kamado-style barbecues with lids on that give you more control over the cooking temperature than a traditional barbecue does. I'm licking my lips at the thought of one! I think I might start saving up my pennies . . .

WHAT MAKES A GOOD BARBECUE?

It you take it down to basics, all a barbecue is, really, is a metal rack held in place over some burning charcoal. It is dead easy to build your own, so long as you've got some bricks, a sturdy metal tray to hold the charcoal, a metal rack that's the same width as the tray to put your bangers, burgers and 'babs on . . . oh, and a smidgeon of common sense.

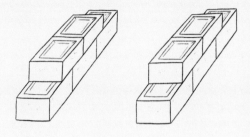

STEP 1

Stack your bricks into two miniature walls so they are a couple of rows high and the gap between them is a bit narrower than the metal tray and rack.

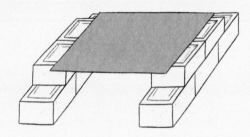

STEP 2

Place the metal tray on top, and take the time to shift the bricks a little if need be so that the tray is level and secure.

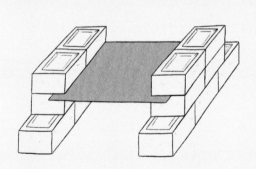

STEP 3

Stack another row of bricks at each side, trapping the tray in place. Clear the area around you so you've got a safe space when you're ready to light the barbecue.

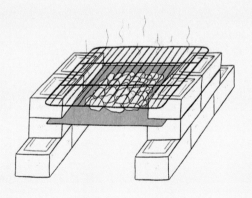

STEP 4

Place charcoal in the metal tray (you'll have to lift the upper rack off to do this), light it and wait for it to burn fiercely and then start to die down. Replace the cooking rack and get those burgers on there!

Small Spaces

Now, I know what some of you might be thinking. It's all very well me banging on about garden furniture and barbecues, but if you live in a city, your outdoor space may hardly have room to swing a hamster. Is it a waste of time for you to even think of trying to do something cool with it?

Nah, not at all! You can always make the most of precious outdoor space, even if it's only a window box full of herbs or flowers to brighten your vista. If you've got a really small garden, yard or balcony you can still make it feel like a great place to be with a few space-saving tricks – and, most importantly, by personalizing it to make it your own.

HOW TO MAKE A SMALL SPACE LOOK BIGGER

Here's the best hint: get everything you can off the ground. Obviously, you can't do that for a table or chairs (unless they fold up and you have handy hooks on the wall you can hang them from), but you can do this with plant pots, clothes airers, storage units, candles or lights.

Basically, whatever you want in your outdoor space that doesn't need to stand on the floor should be attached to your walls, railings or fences. Believe me, the more terra firma you can clock, the bigger your space will feel.

MAXIMUM FLEXIBILITY

I've already mentioned hooks on the wall and folding chairs, but the other thing to consider is wheels. These are ideal for spaces that are compact but not tiny, and where you might want a bit more growing space than you get in planters attached to the wall.

What about a big wooden planter on wheels? It's great because it can be centrestage when you want something pretty to look at, but then you can shove it to one side if you want more space to hang out or eat. It's also great for your plants, as you can push them into the sun or shade, depending on what is required at the time.

RECEDING WALLS

Much as I'd love to tell you to put your walls on wheels and give them a push to increase your space, I don't think your neighbours would be too happy with this arrangement. Spoilsports! But there are other ways to make your garden or yard feel larger. You can use colour to create the illusion of more space. If you paint your fence or walls in a light, cool shade such as pale blue, you'll instantly make your outside area look bigger.

Make sure you buy outdoor paint that's appropriate for whatever your fence or wall is made of. As long as you do that, it should last for a good few years before it needs a new coat.

KEEP IT SIMPLE

Keep different colours to a minimum and stick to similar shapes for all of your outdoor furniture, planters, lighting, etc. If everything co-ordinates well the space will look clean and clear. You can enhance this by not packing too much stuff in there. Choose a few essentials and give them room to breathe.

That goes for your plants, too. A riot of colour may well be just the look you crave, but bear in mind that loads of different textures, sizes and colours in your planting will make the space visually much busier, which in turn will make it look smaller, or even claustrophobic.

Having said all that, you'd think I'd have no time for any garden gnomes cluttering up the place. The truth is, though, I've got a secret soft spot for the odd gnome or two. Let's just call it a guilty pleasure and keep it between ourselves, eh?

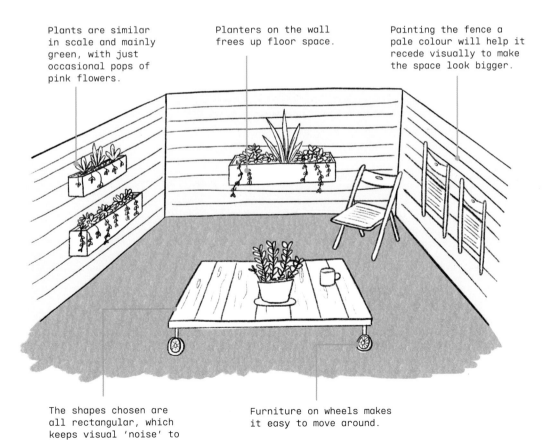

Plants are similar in scale and mainly green, with just occasional pops of pink flowers.

Planters on the wall frees up floor space.

Painting the fence a pale colour will help it recede visually to make the space look bigger.

The shapes chosen are all rectangular, which keeps visual 'noise' to a minimum.

Furniture on wheels makes it easy to move around.

Sheds and their cousins

I must admit that I'm not a huge fan of garden sheds, on aesthetic grounds. Even so, I appreciate that they're a neat way to store all of your garden essentials. Just make sure your shed doesn't become a general dumping ground for stuff you don't really need to keep.

My absolute top tip for your shed? Keep it organized! As with any storage space, you need to be able to get to everything you need as easily as possible and to see where things are. You don't want to be walking into rakes in the dark like Mr Magoo!

THE CLASSIC GARDEN SHED

We all know what this looks like. A simple shape with a pitched roof so that the rain runs off it easily. Sizes vary, but there are loads of options in garden centres, shed centres and online if you're looking to install or replace one.

Traditionally, these are made from wood, which can be painted with wood preservative or paint to help it last longer (and look nicer). The roof is covered with a flexible sheet of roofing felt that contains bitumen, making it waterproof and tough.

When it comes to your shed, the key thing is to figure out what needs to be stored in there and where it will all fit the best. Installing shelves, hooks, or some beams across the top of the walls helps with storing things in a sensible way and keeping them in decent nick.

GREENHOUSES

I'll admit that my fingers are not green, so I don't personally have much call for a greenhouse to grow plants in, but if you think about it, greenhouses can have way more uses than just for plants. They're cool to look at and can work as great all-weather outdoor social spaces, too.

This is crucial: if you want to install a greenhouse in your garden, you must think about where to put it in terms of light, shade and what you will be growing in there. So, visit a few gardening websites, do your research and make a plan.

GARDEN OFFICES

Now this is much more up my street! I was a big fan of having a garden office long before the Covid lockdowns that saw an incredible surge in demand for them. Suddenly, people were finding they had to work from home, regardless of whether they had the space to do so or not.

Without getting all feng shui here, I don't believe it's great for your wellbeing to be working in the kitchen, bedroom or front room. They're spaces to relax and gather together in. It's far healthier to 'go' to work outside your four walls, even if the commute to your garden office only takes three seconds.

⟫ Isn't a garden office just a clean shed?

If only that were true – they'd be so much easier and cheaper to install!

The key differences between sheds and garden offices are to do with insulation, light, power and internet access. A basic garden shed needs to be dry, waterproof and ventilated so things don't go mouldy. And that's it – sorted!

By contrast, a garden office needs to be all of those things plus it needs to be warm in winter and cool in summer (hence needing insulation); it needs natural daylight as well as electric light (so windows and power); and it requires sockets to power your computer as well as decent internet access. After all, you may need to be on emails and video call meetings all day long.

Jay's
Top Tip

Remember that garden offices need to be kept neat and tidy too! It's no use investing in a great space to work in if you end up surrounded by clutter. A desk with drawers and some shelves on the wall for files or reference materials all help to make it a really functional AND good-looking space.

›› Planning a garden office

First check with your local council whether you will need planning permission. They will have information on their website about the rules in place in your area, with guidance on the maximum size and height of a building that you can construct without having to get planning permission.

Although most garden offices are separate buildings, you're going to need to run a hefty electric cable down there and probably a cable for the internet too. Talk to an electrician, early doors, to see whether where you stick your office will impact on the price of connecting it up to your house, and how you can do this without too much disruption to your garden.

›› Choosing the right option for you and your budget

There are a lot of companies out there who will come and install a garden office for you. If you're short on time, and have the budget, then great! Job's a good 'un! But unless you don't mind burning cash, do your research first. Get quotes from several companies, and, ideally, find a local firm – they tend not to have overheads of national advertising and swanky showrooms to pay for. Plus, you're supporting a local independent business. What's not to like?

If you're not so cash-rich, you can do a lot of the work yourself. Just be aware that you'll need to lay a base (usually concrete), which has to be perfectly level and true; install the wall and roof panels; hang the door . . . It's a lot of graft, and you will need physical help.

You might be able to go a middle way. What about finding a local builder who will install a garden office that you purchase as a DIY kit? That can be a really budget-friendly option, although of course it requires a little more of your time and energy to source the right product and person to help you. And don't forget the electrician to get you wired up and connected to your home's power!

PLAYHOUSES

Does it feel like planning your garden is all work and no play? Well, it doesn't have to be! If you have the space, and kids or grandkids on the scene, a playhouse or treehouse can be a really fun thing to have.

On the most basic level, making playhouses out of cardboard boxes is great fun for an afternoon, and a good way to teach some rudimentary construction skills to the next generation. Or you might want to go a bit upmarket and buy a wooden playhouse that comes as a kit. That way, you know it will be safe, the doors will align and the timber will be smooth and splinter-free.

Of course, getting the kids to help with construction and any painting you might do will help them feel it's really theirs. They'll get the same sense of pride that you get from doing successful DIY, and the more involved they are, the more they'll want to use it.

TREEHOUSES

If you're lucky enough to have a sturdy tree in your garden, a treehouse may just be the best thing ever for your kids. You do need to make sure that this adventure isn't going to result in you all ending up down A&E, though, so get some good advice on the health of your tree before you go ahead!

Before you decide on the exact height and dimensions of what will work in your garden, have a butcher's at the playground equipment in your local park. Look at the height, the flooring, the steps to get up there. Most playground apparatus is very cleverly designed so that little kids can't get up the steps or ladders to heights that could be dangerous for them. Measure, make notes and follow the same logic for your garden.

It goes without saying (but I'll say it anyway) that you need to ensure whatever you build is strong, sturdy and supervised by an adult when the kids are out there. Always play it safe, but be sure to have fun!

Up *the* Garden Path

A path can really change the overall look of your garden. This is especially true if you use interesting materials and make it curve or zig-zag all the way down the garden. And, if you've got a garden office to walk to in winter, it can save you a lot of grotty floor-cleaning hassle!

Keen gardeners might choose to have tons of flowerbeds with grassy 'lawn paths' in between them. Fair enough, each to their own, but I am personally more inclined to have something more hardwearing than grass to serve as my path.

PATH MATERIALS

There are so many choices of path materials that it can be hard to know where to start. Well, if you're feeling overwhelmed by multiple options, try matching your path material to another element of your garden for a coherent look.

Have you got brick walls? Try adding a brick path. Do you have railway sleepers round your flower beds? Cut-down sleepers make excellent 'stepping stone' paths. A paved patio area? Set some of the slabs into your lawn.

You also need to think about the purpose the path will serve, and what might not work for your situation. Got dogs who love to dig? Gravel isn't your best option. Is your path going to be purely functional, to get you to your garden office with the cleanest shoes possible? If so, avoid messy bark chippings!

Here are some of the most popular choices for making paths:

GRAVEL

This is probably the cheapest material, but it will need topping up every five years or so. Before you add the gravel, you'll need to dig out the pathway to the depth of the gravel you are pouring in and line it with a weed-suppressing membrane – otherwise you'll end up with lots of weeds popping their heads up where you don't want them.

Happily, there are loads of different types of gravel, in all different sizes and colours, so you have plenty of options when it comes to the overall look and feel of your path.

PAVING SLABS

These work really well in conjunction with gravel or simply by themselves. Just be sure to install them properly and bed them in so that you don't have wobbly slabs or a trip hazard.

BARK CHIPPINGS (ALSO KNOWN AS MULCH)

This is a really environmentally friendly option if you source the mulch locally, but it will need topping up every year or so as it rots down. The best thing: you don't have to dig a base for this sort of path, so you can skip the aching back!

STEPPING STONES

The 'stones' can be made of slate, wood, stone, concrete, recycled tyres – basically, anything hardwearing. As with the paving slabs, you'll need to install them carefully so they are solid, secure and level with the ground.

GRASS (REAL OR ARTIFICIAL)

This can be a great way of getting some grass into an otherwise lawn-free garden. If you expect a lot of foot traffic up and down the path, fake grass is the best option so you don't end up with a mud-bath.

BRICKS

Bricks make great paths. You can lay them in different patterns to suit the look of your garden. Over time, you may get little plants growing in the cracks between them, but this can actually enhance the look of a cottage-style garden, if that's what twists your melon.

PATH SIZE AND SHAPE

Think about how you want the path to look, and who will be using it. If someone in your household is in a wheelchair, for example, you'll need to make sure any garden path is suitable for the chair's wheels in terms of materials and also make sure it is the right width.

The shape of the path is up to you, but sketch out your ideas and options first so that you can see how different forms change the overall look of the garden. A straight path can look pretty boring . . . or really modern and striking. A meandering path can look more interesting, or it can irritate you if you have to walk down it twenty times a day. Horses for courses! As with all of my advice in this book, think it through and take your time to figure out what will work best for you and your household. Get your grey matter working and planning. It will be worth it.

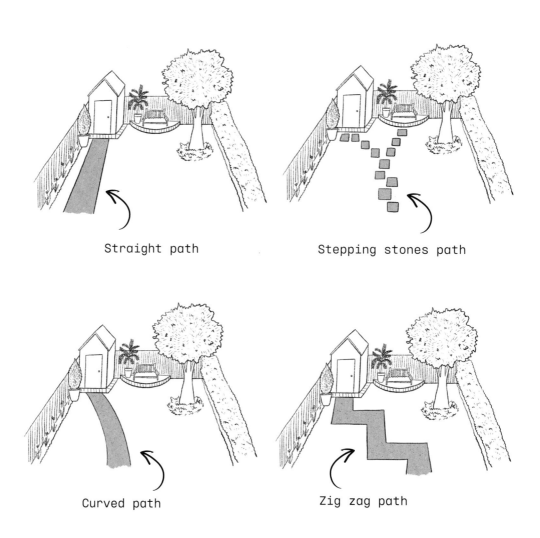

Straight path

Stepping stones path

Curved path

Zig zag path

Garden Lighting

I love using lights to create interest and atmosphere. These days, you can get all sorts of different garden lights, and many of them are solar-powered, which are easier to install than mains-powered lights, and even better for your wallet and the environment. The only drawback is that solar-powered lights need a fair bit of sun, so don't rely on them too heavily unless you live somewhere with plenty of sunshine every day! (I'm sure there must be places like that in Britain, although I can't think where they are right now!)

WARM OR COOL LIGHT?

White is white, right? Wrong! Believe it or not, there are loads of different types of white lights available. They all fit along a spectrum from a really yellowy white at one end to a bright, blue-ish white at the other.

The warmness or coolness of the light is measured in units called kelvins. A warm white might say 2500k on the packaging or on the specification; a cool white might say 7000k. Basically, the higher the number, the cooler the white. So, 4000k is roughly equivalent to moonlight, which is fairly neutral.

A good rule of thumb is to opt for warmer lighting in social spaces where you'll be lighting people, and cooler white when you want to showcase your plants.

ENOUGH BUT NOT TOO MUCH

When it comes to light levels, you want to be able to see, but you don't want to dazzle people, animals and insects – or your neighbours! If you have a medium-to-large garden it's best to have several different light options. This gives you a degree of nuance in your lighting scheme. I doubt you'll want to light up the entire garden as though you're having a full-on party when you're just taking the bins out!

CANDLES AND TORCHES

I'm a big fan of candles and candlelight. It can look great in the garden so long as you've got some decent holders that will keep the wind from blowing out the flames. Oil-burning garden torches can look well dramatic as well, especially if you use a row of them to light a path. Never leave burning candles or torches unattended, and keep kids away from them.

Patios & Decking

Let's get this out there before we say another word. Any plans that you make for your outdoor spaces will always have to make allowances for our great (ahem!) British weather.

With this is mind, it's a good idea to have an area of garden closest to the house that dries fast when the rain stops. If you have to step out of your back door straight onto grass you'll constantly be tramping mud into the house – or you'll barely set foot in your garden. What a mess! What a waste of space!

Decking is a great solution. I've installed my own in the past but, without blowing my own trumpet, bear in mind that I worked for years as a builder before I got into telly. The truth is, laying decking is hard work, and you really have to get the underframe perfectly level, with joists correctly spaced, if your deck is going to be safe and long-lasting.

SPRUCING UP A PATIO

Pressure-washing can work wonders on a patio that's looking in a bit of a two-and-eight. You can hire pressure washers fairly cheaply, but a word of warning – don't underestimate the amount of gunk that will spray up and onto your legs!

What to do if you've cleaned your patio and still don't like how it looks? First of all, don't despair! If you've got a clean, level surface, there are plenty of things you can do to try to get it looking more presentable.

What about adding some durable outdoor paint? Even dodgy eighties-style crazy paving can look OK with a coat or two of paint in a colour that suits the rest of the house and garden. Think about what will work well with your plants and fences or walls.

Another idea is to put decking tiles on top of the patio. These are available in different grades and finishes to suit their intended use and your budget. Or how about adding an outdoor rug? And there's a bonus: these are often made from recycled plastic so are environmentally friendly.

LOOKING AFTER YOUR TIMBER DECKING

Ventilation is very important so getting it installed properly (or installing it properly yourself) is key so that the underframe doesn't go rotten, not to mention the boards themselves.

Make sure you sweep your decking regularly, moving any outdoor furniture or plant pots out of the way and getting underneath them. If you have any algae or moss growing on the deck, it's important to remove these. Jet-washing can work well, or a good scrub with decking cleaner.

To keep everything spick and span, apply decking oil every few years. It really helps to preserve the wood and give your deck a longer lifespan, and it isn't hard to do. Just follow the manufacturer's instructions and you'll be laughing!

Jay's Top Tip

If you have plant pots on your patio or decking, prop them up on plant pot 'feet' or small bricks. That way, the wood can still breathe and you won't get a small insect farm developing under the pot.

Fences, Walls & Hedges

I know hedges are great for wildlife, but for me they are way too much of a palaver. If you've got the time and the patience for regular hedge-trimming over the summer months then I take my hat off to you, Sir or Madam. Me, I prefer fences.

Why? Well, they're easy to install (easier than building a wall or waiting for a hedge to grow, anyway!), relatively cheap (I ask you, have you seen the price of bricks?) and you have the option of painting them in any colour you like. I'm not on the fence: I'm on Team Fence!

FENCES AND WIND?

There is, admittedly, the issue that fences have a bit of a reputation for coming down in the wind. However, this really depends on the type of fence and how it's been installed. It's definitely an avoidable problem with a bit of planning.

If your fence has gaps for the air to flow through, it's much less likely that it'll be blown down in a storm. Think about it: sails on a ship are solid sheets of material, which makes them really good at catching the wind and using its power to move the vessel along. What would happen if there were holes in the sheet? The boat would barely move!

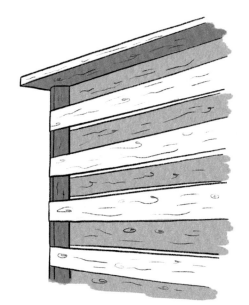

The same principle applies to your fence. Attach the horizontal planks between the fence posts so that they alternate from front to back. It makes a decent air gap, but it's not so big that you end up gawping at your next-door neighbour as they do their gardening at the weekend!

GARDEN WALLS

There's no denying that a wall is your most solid option. However, building a new wall properly and safely requires digging foundations to make sure the wall stays where it's been built.

That said, if you've got the budget, even a low wall can make a great base for wooden or metal fence panels on top, then you can create something strong and durable without making your home look like a maximum-security prison.

If you've moved into a gaff with a garden wall that's looking a bit shabby, get it looked at by a builder. As long as it's solid, it might be repairable, or it might just need re-pointing between the bricks. If it's structurally ok but you hate the look of it, you can always paint it!

HEDGES

OK, I guess I've got to accept that even after Jay's words of wisdom some of you out there are still going to want a garden hedge, or perhaps you have one that you need to spruce up a bit. Well, if I can't talk you out of it, here's the best way to sort it.

Firstly, and most importantly, make sure you keep it looking neat and tidy. Don't let it get overgrown to the point where it's causing an obstruction on the pavement or road outside. It's anti-social and it ain't gonna make you popular in the neighbourhood!

The classic hedge choice is privet. This is very hardy and doesn't need much in the way of care. But even without being a hedge expert, I know there are plenty more interesting options out there. So, go down to your local garden centre, find a friendly assistant and have a word in their shell-like. They'll probably be happy to help. Just make sure that whatever foliage you choose is going to look good all year round. And if you get a hedge that sheds its leaves once a year, get ready to clear those away! (See, I told you hedges are hard work didn't I? Don't say I never warned you . . .)

My Favourite...

GARDEN SEATING

Some DIY jobs are precisely planned from start to finish, others come about by chance, or even from a mistake – and the funny thing is, these can end up being the ones that you are the proudest of.

A few years back, I was laying decking around my house and I cut a few planks to size. My plan was to run decking up to the house, but I'd cut my planks too short! I let out a big sigh but then a light bulb came on over my head – Ting!

'Hold up, Jay! You can do something really clever here!' I realized that I could build seating against the house wall that could double as storage space. It was a simple idea, really, but you know what they say about simple ideas: they're usually the best!

I left the slightly short decking on the ground where it was and used some more planks to build the seat, running up against the house wall and covering the gap in the decking base. The seats looked like a box, so I measured carefully to get the front and top pieces exactly the right size. But the seats didn't just look like a box: they were a box! I used hinges, like you find on a garden gate, so you could lift up the top of the seats, then I put plastic membrane inside to keep the rain out. Ta-da! A new seating area with bonus storage!

Man, I loved that decking area. We had so many fun barbecues in that garden and we could cram loads of stuff in the seats: garden tools, deckchairs, Zola's inflatable toys – we even managed to fit the lawnmower in!

I won't pretend building decking seating was a quick-and-easy job: working on my tod, it took me two weeks. Moral of the tale? Don't be afraid to make the odd mistake – it might lead somewhere interesting!

index

A
alcoves 68–9, 188–9, 202–5
Artex 40
asbestos 40, 43

B
bags, storing 142, 144
banisters 126–7
barbecues 237, 246–7
baskets, as bedside storage 195
bath mats 152
bathroom 152–89
    flooring 168–75
    lights 186–7
    plumbing 176–83
    silicone sealant 176–7
    storage 188–9
    taps 180–3
    tiles 156–69
beanbags 102, 244
bedroom 192–231
    bedhead/footboard 230–1
    beds 226–31
    blinds 220–1
    carpet/rugs 206–13
    curtains 214–19
    doors 224–5
    shutters 222–3
    storage 195–205
bicycles, storing 142, 144
blankets 110–11
blinds 202, 220–1
blowtorch 28, 29
boxes, storage 140, 143, 200
breezeblocks 32, 116
bricks 32
    barbecues 247
    kitchen cupboards 64, 66
    paths 254, 255
bug hotels 237
buggies, storing 142, 143, 144
bunk beds 227, 229

C
candles 101, 114, 186, 195, 248, 257
carpet 206–11
    tiles 56, 62
ceilings 38, 40–1, 91, 92–3
chairs

garden 242–4
kitchen 78, 80–3
living room 86, 90, 103–7
renovating 47, 80–3, 106–7
chalk line tool 25
chests 200
chipboard 34
closets see wardrobes
clothing
    built-in storage 202–5
    in hallways 142, 144
    storage 200–5
    walk-in closets 195
    wardrobes 196–7
    workwear 43
colour schemes
    accent colours 108
    artwork link 82–3
    small spaces 248–9
cork tiles 56, 62
cracks, filling 92
cupboards
    kitchen 64–7, 195
    renovating 47
    see also storage
curtains 214–19
    attachments 217
    as door alternative 202
    draughtproofing 146
    fitting 32, 217
    poles 214, 216, 217
    tiebacks/holdbacks 218
    track 216, 217
curves
    cutting tiles 166
    sawing 45
cushions
    covers 108–9
    floor 102
    garden furniture 244, 264
    pads 108

D
decals 98
decking 234, 258–9, 264
dog leads 142, 144
doorframes, painting 93
doors
    cupboard 66–7

external 120, 146–7, 238–9, 241
internal 224–5
wardrobe 197, 202, 205, 230
draughtproofing 146, 147, 224
drawers
chest of 198–9
fixing problems 198
renovating 47
as storage 140
under stairs 148–9
drills 22, 23

F
fences 240, 260
fireplaces 112–15
floors/flooring
bathrooms 168–75
ceramic tiles 168, 171
cleaning/repairing 172
construction 38–9
kitchen 56–63
laminate/engineered wood 60–1
painting 56–8
sanding floorboards 59
soft floor tiles 62–3, 171
vinyl 171, 172, 174–5
wooden 58–9, 61, 171
furniture
garden 242–5, 248, 249, 264–5
living room 86, 90, 102–11
recycling 47

G
garden
back gardens 234, 242
barbecues 237, 246–7
decking 234, 258–9, 264
fences/walls/hedges 260–3
front gardens 234, 238, 240–1
garden offices 234, 237, 251–2, 254
lighting 240, 257
paths 254–6
plants 248, 249, 259
playhouses 252–3
seating 237, 242–5, 264–5
sheds 250
storage 237, 248, 250, 264–5
see also outdoor spaces

glass
external doors 147
shelves 68, 116
splashbacks 75
'green' materials 37, 47, 156, 158, 211

greenhouses 251
grouting 156, 158, 168

H
hallways 120–49
pictures 132–9
storage 140–5
woodwork 124–31
hammers 20, 21
hammocks 244
hand tools 20–7, 43
handles, changing 47, 197, 238
hanging rails 200, 202
hardboard 34
headboard 230–1
health and safety 6
ceilings 40
lead-based paint 43, 59, 128
rugs 212
sawing/sanding 34, 59
using tools/equipment 6, 42–3
heat gun 28, 29, 46
hedges 240, 260, 262
hinges 67
hooks 31, 138–9, 142–3

I
insulation materials 34

J
joists 38, 39

K
keys, storing 140, 144
kitchen 50–83
chairs 78, 80–3
cupboards 64–7, 195
flooring 56–63
planning 54–5
shelves 68–71
sinks 72–3, 76
tables 78–9, 82–3
worktops 72–3
knives, utility 24

L
ladders, using 43
letterboxes 147
level 20, 21
lights
bathroom 186–7
ceiling centrepiece 41
decorating round switches 91, 97, 98
garden 234, 240, 257

LED ideas 75, 126
living room 100–1
linoleum 171
lintels 32
living room 86–117
    cushions & blankets 108–10
    decals/posters/murals 98
    fireplaces 112–15
    furniture 86, 90, 102–11
    lighting 100–1
    music systems 116–17
    painting 91–3
    planning 90
    wallpaper 94–7
locks 146–7

M
magnet 22, 23
mail, dealing with 140, 144
masks, wearing 34, 59
materials 22–3, 32–4, 37, 47
matresses 228
MDF 34
measuring 20
mirrors 132–3, 138–9, 142, 200
mould, removing from sealant 176–7
mouldings 41
murals 98
music systems 116–17, 195, 234

N
nails 22, 23, 30

O
outdoor spaces 234–67
    front of house 238–41
    seating 237, 242–5, 264–5
    small gardens 248–9
    see also garden

P
paint/painting
    ceilings 91, 92–3
    cleaning woodwork 124–5

    doors 93, 224
    flooring 56–8
    lead-based 43, 59, 128
    living room 91–3
    patios 258
    removing 46, 58–9, 128, 161
    tile paint 160–1
    wardrobes 196–7
    woodwork 93, 128–30

paths 254–6
patios 258–9
pencils 20, 21
pictures, hanging 132–9
planning 54–5, 90, 94, 252
plaster 34, 92
plasterboard fixings 31
playhouses 252
pliers 24
plumb bob 25
plumbing
    bathroom 176–83
    kitchen 77
    PTFE tape 76
plywood 34, 73
power tools 28–9, 43, 46
professional help
    Artex ceilings 40
    carpentry 224
    carpet fitting 208
    electricity 42, 43, 186, 252
    plastering 34
    plumbing 77, 182
    reupholstery 106
    structural work 37, 92, 114, 171, 252
pull cord switches 186
putty knife 25

R
recycling/reusing/repurposing 47
    beds 13, 226, 230–1
    internal doors 224
    kitchen cupboards 64
    shelving 10
    tables and chairs 78, 80–3
    wardrobes 10, 13, 196–7
roof windows, blinds 222
rugs 206, 212–13, 258

S
sanders 28, 29
sanding 45, 59
sawing curves 45
saws 25, 28, 29

scissors/shears 24
scrapers 25
scratches, in flooring 172
screwdriver 22, 23
screws 22, 23, 30
scribing worktops 44–5
seating, garden 237, 242–5, 264–5
    see also chairs; sofas
security 140, 146–7, 240

sewing 106–7, 108–9, 111
sheds 250
shelving
    bathrooms 152, 188–9
    glass 68, 116
    hallways 143
    kitchen 68–71
    music systems 116–17
shoes, storing 140, 144
showers 152, 155
shutters 222–3
silicone sealant 176–7
sinks
    bathroom taps 180–3
    blockages 180
    kitchen 72–3, 76
skirting boards 93, 124–5
sofas
    garden 244, 245
    living room 86, 102–5
    updating 47, 106–7
spanner 22, 23
splashbacks 54, 74–5
staircases 120–49
    banisters 126–7
    stairgates 147
    storage 148–9
staple gun 24
steamers 46
storage
    bathroom 188–9
    bedroom 195–205
    built-in 202–5
    DIY materials 22, 23
    garden 237, 248, 250, 264–5
    hallways 140–5, 148–9
stud/cable detector 25, 30, 32
sugar soap 58
swing seats 244

T
tables, kitchen 78–9
tape measure 20, 21
taps, bathroom 180–3

techniques 42–6
television 86, 90, 195
textiles, as wall decoration 99
tile cutter 25, 166
tiles
    bathrooms 156–69
    carpet 56, 62
    ceiling 40
    cleaning 158, 176

cutting 44, 166
flooring 168, 171
grouting 156, 158, 168
painting 160–1
replacing cracked 158–9
splashbacks 74
vinyl 62–3, 171
wall tiles 162–7
worktops 73
toilets 155, 184–5
tools and equipment 20–31, 43
treehouses 253
trunks 200

umbrellas 142, 144
underlay 208–9
upholstery 80–1, 104–7

V
ventilation 43

W
wall plugs 31
wallpaper
    on furniture/doors 197, 224
    living room 94–7
    stripping 46, 91
walls 34, 36–7
    filling cracks 92
    garden 240, 248–9, 262
    murals 98
    painting 91–3
    shelves 68–71
    tiling 162–7
    wall cupboards 64, 67, 200
    wall-mounted table 78–9
wardrobes 196–7
    built-in 202–5
    renovating 196–7
    walk-in 195
water, finding/fixing leaks 178–83
wildlife, encouraging 237
windows 222, 240, 241
woodwork, painting 93, 124–31
worktops 44–5, 72–3
wrench 22, 23

Thanks *for* Reading!

I hope this book helps you on your way to being a DIY champion! Just remember that with some thought, planning and careful measuring you too can become a seasoned home improvements guru, and you might even inspire your friends and family to have a go as well. Don't forget to let me know how you get on!

@jaybladesmbe
#DIYwithJay

I wish you every success!

ALSO BY JAY BLADES MBE

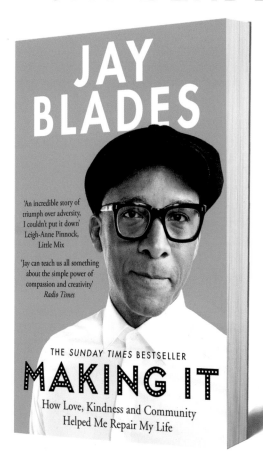

THE SUNDAY TIMES BESTSELLER
MAKING IT

How Love, Kindness and Community Helped Me Repair My Life

'An incredible story of triumph over adversity, I couldn't put it down.'
– Leigh-Anne Pinnock, Little Mix

*'Jay can teach us all something about the simple power
of compassion and creativity.'* – Radio Times

Making It is an inspirational memoir about beating the odds and turning
things around even when it all seems hopeless, by Jay Blades, the beloved
star of hit BBC One show *The Repair Shop*.

AVAILABLE IN PAPERBACK, EBOOK AND AUDIO

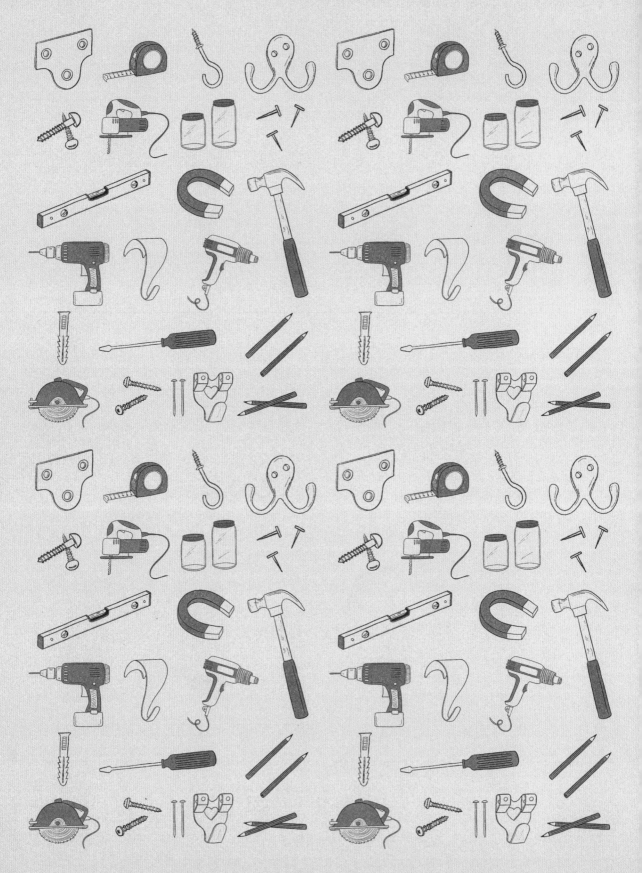